Revenge:

How to Beat the

Narcissist

By

H G Tudor

Copyright 2016

Revenge:

How to Beat the Narcissist

By

HG Tudor

Published by Insight Books

1. Introduction

If you want to achieve revenge over a narcissist there is only one person who can explain how to do this. The narcissist. That is because in order to exact revenge, true and proper revenge you need to understand what the narcissist fears more than anything and what will destroy the narcissist. Only the narcissist knows this. Only the narcissist can detail to you what it is that will achieve revenge and the methodology you will have to apply to secure this. Nobody else can help you do this. Others will have suggestions. Others will detail ways of countering our behaviours. That is not revenge. That is containing us. There are those who will advocate No Contact. No Contact secures almost complete freedom from our kind but it is not revenge. To achieve real revenge, you must heed the words of the narcissist. My words.

Revenge. Getting your own back. Getting one over on the enemy. Just desserts. Justice. Call it what you will these are all forms of revenge and at some point in our lives we will have experienced that burning desire to exact revenge on somebody who has caused a problem. It might by minor, for instance the first time somebody has pinched a toy from us at school as an infant and we want to get them back for it. It may become the desire to get revenge over somebody who has excluded us from a group of friends at school. It may be an instant response and one, which can be executed in a moment, such as winning the ball back at football after having been tackled. As we become older the basis for and the scale of seeking revenge increases. No longer do we seek a favourable outcome following some petty slight committed against us. We do not want justice for the theft of our sweets. The stakes have increased. We want revenge on the person who beat us unfairly to that promotion at work. We want revenge on the neighbour who plays loud music late at night and keeps us awake. We want revenge on the person who stole our boyfriend or girlfriend away from us. We want revenge for the bullying of our child or the unfair treatment of a relative. Revenge is a common and normal emotional response.

When you have suffered at the hands of a narcissist it is highly likely that you will experience a thirst for revenge. This desire is driven by the awful treatment that he or she meted out against you. The months if not years of repeated abuse, the silent treatments, the beatings, the put-downs, the disappointments and so on. All delivered against a backdrop of hypocrisy, contradiction, lack of responsibility and blame shifting. You have been put through the ringer. The cost to you may have been high. There is always a cost for the victims of the narcissist. Always you will have faced an emotional cost as you are left bewildered by what has happened to you. You are wondering why it had to happen to you and what was that you have done to deserve such treatment? You may be traumatised exhibiting the symptoms of post traumatic stress disorder such was the severity of the treatment that you have been subjected to. Your sanity may hang by a thread. The damage does not just end there. You may have lost friends, fallen out with family and face significant financial difficulties after the destructive tornado that is the narcissist has passed through your life. You may have lost your job or now be too ill to work. You may have seen prized possessions stolen or destroyed. Faced a terrible fight through the courts involving your children. Every facet of your life has been affected by this insidious creature, which arrived with love and affection and then in an instant turned into the devil. He or she will not even be done with you. Despite the fact they have left you dazed and confused in the gutter, the narcissist will still keep coming back, pulling your strings and looking to Hoover you back into his or her nightmare existence in order to extract some fuel from you. You cannot be left to piece your life together, lick your wounds and try and move on. The ghoulish narcissist continues to haunt you, preventing your recovery and seeking to administer yet more pain to you despite presenting with faux remorse and contrition.

It may take you some time to realise that you actually became entangled with and even once you realise this, it will take you even longer to process on an emotional level what has happened to you. You require

r̶e̶c̶u̶p̶e̶r̶a̶t̶i̶v̶e̶ ̶s̶u̶p̶p̶o̶r̶t̶ ̶f̶r̶o̶m̶ ̶t̶h̶o̶s̶e̶ ̶s̶u̶p̶p̶o̶r̶t̶ ̶n̶e̶t̶w̶o̶r̶k̶s̶ ̶y̶o̶u̶ ̶m̶a̶y̶ ̶h̶a̶v̶e̶ ̶l̶e̶f̶t̶ ̶a̶f̶t̶e̶r̶

the damage caused by the narcissist. Professional treatment is often required as you try to make sense of what happened, how you became involved in it and allowing all of this to be eradicated from your heart and your head.

Some people focus on putting their life back together, healing and moving on. It is a tough task and with the spectre of the narcissist nearby, it may prove impossible to ever return to the person they were before the emotional vampire swept into their lives. This victim will eventually learn about the application of No Contact and how this doctrine is the only way to ensure that the narcissist is kept at bay and thus they are given time and space to effect as much as a recovery as they can. The implementation and the maintenance of No Contact are difficult and require preparation, perseverance and considerable commitment. If you have not already I recommend you read my book **No Contact: How to Beat the Narcissist** in order to protect yourself and maximise your prospects of successfully applying this concept.

In some respects, you should regard the instigation of No Contact as a form of revenge against the narcissist that has plagued your life. No Contact works on the premise that by denying any contact in absolutely any form with the narcissist you will deprive him or her of fuel. Fuel is the lifeblood of the narcissist. Remove this and you threaten his or her very existence. You may face (dependent on timing and the type of narcissist that you are dealing with) a frenzied attempt to recover this fuel from you. The narcissist will want to destroy your attempt at No Contact, breach your defences and reinstate that precious fuel provision once again. He will deploy manipulation after manipulation in order to try to achieve this. If you maintain No Contact he will be forced to seek this fuel from other sources and thus you will, for the most part be left alone. By denying the narcissist the very thing that he or she wants and moreover needs you will exact a form of revenge against him or her. You will deny them their fuel and force them to go elsewhere to find it, leaving you to recover and put your life back together again. That is truly a form of revenge over the narcissist.

The difficulties involved in implementing and maintaining No Contact mean that should someone succeed in doing this and remove the narcissist from their life (subject to further Hoover attempts) mean that for many people this is as good as it gets. It may not be in their nature to want to do anything more than secure their own freedom and recovery. No matter how badly they have been hurt by the narcissist, no matter the extent to which the narcissist has ruined the victim's life that person decides that they must focus on their own defences. They must secure their own safety, recovery and then they can move forward. It may not just be a case of that being the mindset of the relevant victim. He or she may have suffered such a devastating assault on their person and their life that they do not have the strength to do anything more than implement No Contact and to try to maintain it. Anything beyond this is a bridge too far. The weakened state they have been left in means they are obliged to use what resources they have been left with for the sole purpose of trying to maintain their No Contact. Anything else is too much.

Beyond those who are unable to do more or for a variety of reasons they choose to do no more are those people who have been burned by narcissists but No Contact is not enough. They know this is a form of revenge. They mustered the last elements of their strength and fortitude and they implemented No Contact. They weathered the blitzkrieg that followed as the enraged narcissist fought to recover the precious supply from this intimate primary source. They resisted the narcissist's manipulations as he or she tried to secure that Hoover fuel. This victim stood firm as the narcissist went into over-drive in order to breach the No Contact. It was not easy. Far from it, but their will and their resolve held and once the Grand Hoover had been weathered, they continued to maintain No Contact as their former strength returned. They recovered and as the narcissist tried further standard Hoovers from time to time, this victim was not for falling prey to the narcissist's overtures no matter how sweet they sounded. The repeated Power Plays deployed by the narcissist failed to work and gradually the Hoovers became less frequent and less intense. They never go away in their entirety but with each passing month this victim grew stronger. After what they had been put through they not only wanted to deprive the narcissist of his or her fuel but they wanted something more. They wanted their revenge over the narcissist.

This book examines how, should you be of this mindset, you can achieve revenge over the narcissist that ensnared you. It is far from easy. It requires discipline, planning and a dedication to achieving revenge over a powerful creature that knows you inside out. The narcissist is your nemesis. He or she is an agent that will seek to exact punishment against you and at the same time draw fuel from you. The narcissist has no love, compassion or caring for you. He or she only cares about one thing; fuel. Should you wish to go beyond No Contact and seek revenge against your narcissist you can only do so from a position of strength. What does this mean?

This means that you will need support networks to assist you and to provide you with support, assurance and emotional assistance as you lock horns with the narcissist. You will have seen how hard the narcissist can fight when his or her fuel supply is threatened. You are going further than that. In order to seek revenge, you will threaten the very existence of the narcissist by eradicating what he or she thinks he is only leaving behind what he or she actually is. Such an occurrence is the same as the way you would regard death, to a narcissist. Such an act is fatal to the narcissist. He or she will not physically die but in their minds they may as well have done because you will have brought about the destruction of their construct and what they wanted the world to see. You will then have exposed what they always wish to keep hidden, imprisoned and away from every one else and thus in achieving this you will have achieved revenge. By making the decision to seek revenge you will be engaging with a narcissist that is fighting for his or her very survival and as such you will be subjected to attack, manipulation and even the disappearance of the narcissist in order to frustrate and defeat your attempt at securing revenge.

This is no easy undertaking. To bring about this revenge you must ensure that all elements of your life are on an even keel. Home, employment, family, children, friends, money, health and so forth. These elements and others must be in a sound state for if they are not, the narcissist, who remember knows all your weakness, foibles and vulnerabilities will exploit them in order to derail you mission to achieve revenge. Nothing is off limits to the narcissist and when you seek revenge you turn him or her into a very dangerous beast indeed. This means that if you have a vulnerability it will be seized on in order to force you to give up your attempt. You must ensure that before you commence this that you are in a position of strength. Not only must the above facets be in order but also you must have recovered from your ordeal. You must be in a position where any affection, love, connection or desire for the narcissist has been worn down to the absolute minimum. You can never truly obliterate your feelings for the narcissist. That is what makes them so powerful and so dangerous. Their ability to plant that seed inside of you, which they will try and awaken years later in order to draw you back in. You can never remove this seed but you can ensure that you are sufficiently strong and focussed to deal with its awakening once the narcissist tries to do this.

You cannot seek revenge as you start No Contact. You will not have the strength to achieve it. You cannot seek revenge when you have just weather the Grand Hoover. You will not have sufficient resources to achieve it. You cannot seek revenge when you are replenishing your reserves of determination, self-esteem, critical thinking and self-confidence. The demands by the revenge campaign will prove too great for those depleted resources. I have seen it happen. I have witnessed the foolhardy attempt to exact revenge against me and I have crushed them because they were not prepared, they were not strong enough, they were not recovered enough and most of all because they still loved me and had not processed out the emotional attachment that we create with you.

Your blood may be up when you realise what has happened to you and the desire for revenge will be great. Do not think this desire at such a stage will be sufficient to power you as you seek revenge. It is not. The time to seek revenge is some time after the narcissist has been largely banished from your life. They may appear from time to time with the occasional Hoover. You have got your life back on an even keel. You feel strong. The narcissist rarely enters your thoughts and when he or she does you do not feel love, regret, sorrow or a hankering for the golden period. You feel net to nothing other than a desire for revenge. When you are in this position then and only then do you have the potential to commence the revenge campaign. There are no guarantees that you will succeed but what can be guaranteed is that if you try to achieve revenge at an earlier juncture you will certainly fail.

How do I know all of this? It is because I am a narcissist. In tandem with the awareness and insight I have gained from my work with the good doctors and my natural intellect and sophistication I know what I am. I know what I do and I largely understand why I do it. I know that my kind act in very similar ways because those ways work and are the most effective. Accordingly, I can speak for many of our kind. I also know others of our kind and have observed their behaviours for the purpose of increasing my own knowledge and understanding. I also have had many victims and of those several have sought revenge. I know the process. I know how you will fail but I also know how you will succeed. Not against me of course, I am too wary and brilliant for it ever to be used against me but I am able to explain to you how you can seek revenge against the narcissist that was in your life or rather the narcissist, which almost destroyed your life and will do so if given the chance. I know all about the methods which will have to be deployed and the ways in which the narcissist will fight back. Nobody is better placed than me to explain to you how you might seek revenge. No victim can do this, no third party observing professional, only the narcissist can show you how to seek revenge and in this instance that narcissist is me.

Before you decide that you wish to seek revenge consider that if you have implemented and maintained No Contact then you have come a long way and attained a considerable achievement. Consider whether that is enough. You have caused your narcissist much pain and anguish and you have triumphed by becoming largely free from him or her and sent the narcissist away to plague someone else. Should you quit while you are ahead? There is much to be said for doing so. Your life is near normal again, you feel far better and therefore why would you want to risk being dragged back into the nightmare again? Give careful and considered thought as to why you want revenge, the cost involved and whether you are up to the campaign. The content of this book is for your information only. It is detailed for you to make your own decision as to what you do next. It is not written in order to compel you to take action but rather to furnish you with the relevant information to allow you, as a person in control of your own destiny to make an informed decision as to how you wish to proceed. If, following this consideration you reach the conclusion that you are strong enough to do it, prepared to do it and you feel you must do it then read on and prepare yourself to take revenge on the narcissist.

2. The Core Principle

There is a pervasive principle which you must have regard to at all times
when you are seeking revenge against a narcissist. This principle must be
adhered to permanently since a failure to do so will diminish your prospects
of achieving revenge and will also risk you becoming ensnared again by the
narcissist. In order to be able to understand and apply this Core Principle it
is necessary to spend a short time examining the lifeblood of the narcissist.
His or her fuel. I recommend you familiarise yourself with the content of
my book **Fuel** before seeking revenge. It will give you a fundamental
understanding of what causes the narcissist to function and why he or she
behaves as he or she does.

Fuel is what the narcissist needs in order to function. It allows him or
her to produce the means by which they can continue to appear seductive,
interesting, charismatic and alluring to others. Fuel powers the narcissist so
he or she is able to keep the creature that lurks beneath under lock and key.
Fuel enables the projection of what the narcissist wants the world to see and
keeps hidden that which he or she does not want the world to witness.
Without Fuel the narcissist loses the power to charm. Without Fuel the
narcissist is unable to keep the creature under control and faces being
consigned to oblivion. Accordingly, the provision of fuel is of paramount
importance to the narcissist. He or she must harvest fuel on a daily basis.
We need a primary source, which will be somebody we engage in a
relationship with so that we know we have a steady source of high quality
fuel on tap. This however is never enough. We need to seek out fuel for
other sources. These are the supplementary sources and they are varied.
Supplementary sources cover anybody and everybody from strangers to
friends, colleagues to family members and from acquaintances to other
intimate partners. People, who we regard as nothing more than an appliance

for the provision of fuel, are the supplementary sources and this is why we must engage we a variety of different people. It also explains that whomever we may come into contact with during the course of the day we see as a viable target from which we will extract fuel.

What is this fuel? It is emotion infused attention. You will be familiar with our constant need to be centre stage and star of the show. This is because we want attention. We demand and require everybody's attention, yours, hers, his and theirs. We can never get enough of this attention. In order for the attention to qualify as fuel however it needs to be infused with emotion. Those emotions can be either positive or negative. For instance, in respect of positive fuel an admiring glance, a teasing smile, a declaration of love, a praising comment or a warm hug are all aspects of positive fuel. Analysing that further, let's categorise how these each equate to fuel.

Act/Words	Why Positive	Emotion
Glance	Admiring	Appreciation/Envy
Smile	Teasing	Sexual
Declaration	Love	Love
Comment	Praise	Happiness
Hug	Warm	Love/Affection

We always draw positive fuel from our primary source when we first seduce them. We also largely draw positive fuel from our supplementary sources because this is part of maintaining the façade that we are a brilliant, charismatic and likeable person. We do not want the supplementary sources to think to the contrary so we usually ensure that we draw positive fuel from them. We may occasionally, should one of those supplementary sources criticise us, switch to taking negative fuel from them instead. We also, during the course of a day will take negative fuel from those people we do not often interact with, for example a waitress or parking attendant. That is why you will often see the narcissist behave in a high-handed and arrogant manner towards these people. It is all part of drawing the negative fuel.

Negative fuel is similarly based on words or acts but those, which are infused with negative emotions such as fear, upset, anger or frustration. We actually draw a higher quality of fuel by extracting negative fuel and this is why we always devalue those who are in the position of being our primary source of fuel. Once their positive supply starts to wane and it always does, we will then unleash our devaluation to draw the negative fuel from them.

Some people find it odd that we are perfectly content to receive a dressing down as out intimate partner shouts at us and call us names. This is not an issue for us. Although we hear what you are saying we are not listening to the actual words that you are using. The insults and slurs pass us by. We are focussed on the attention you are giving us by engaging in this tirade and also the emotion surrounding it. By standing there screaming at us with tears running down your cheeks as you describe how awful and terrible we are, we are drinking deep of the fuel that is flowing from you. We want your attention and we want it wrapped up in emotion. Should your attention as our primary source move elsewhere or we are not receiving attention from supplementary sources not be paying us the attention we demand we will take steps to remedy the situation. This is why narcissists are often regarded as drama queens. This is why we always ruin birthdays and Christmas and special occasions for other people because we cannot stand to allow someone else to have the limelight even for a moment. It must always be about us. We must have eyes trained on us and whether they shine with admiration or burn with disdain we care not so long as they do and provide us with fuel.

Accordingly, fuel is fundamental to us. The nature of this fuel must be understood in order to apply the Core Principle, which is

A revenge campaign must be administered devoid of emotion

This Core Principle must be adhered to in every dealing that you with us if you are seeking revenge. The moment you fail to apply it then you are not effecting revenge but you are providing us with fuel. This will make us stronger and allow us to lash out at you. Giving us this fuel will provide us with power to find more. It will allow us to shine and attract. It will put the creature back in its place and your hard work so far will start to become undone.

You might be tempted to turn up where we live and howl like a banshee as you put the windows through on our car. Yes, we will react to your conduct but not because we are upset. Far from it. In point of fact we are delighted by your emotional appearance. All that yelling and screaming, the heightened emotional state that you are in and they are all directed at us through our property. It is marvellous. Keep it flowing. We will chastise you and call you a nut job and such like but this is purely done to provoke you further so you keep providing us with fuel. We may appear angry with you smashing the windows on our BMW but we are not, we are savouring and relishing all the fuel you are giving to us. We are triumphant because this exhibits how powerful we are. We can still cause you to feel this way (good or bad) about us and this reinforces our sense of omnipotence. The worst things you can ever do to us are ignore us, be ambivalent about us or act as if we do not exist. Such behaviour wounds us. Do anything, anything at all which is directed at us and unleashes your emotions and then you are exhibiting how powerful we are. We have a hold over you. We value negative responses over positive ones because they are harder to achieve and their manifestation is validation of the sheer scale of our power over you. You may want to go nuclear on us because of what we have done, you may want to shout, and scream and holler, but all you are doing is playing into our hands.

When you begin your revenge campaign each step, each act and every interaction with us must be done in a sterile manner. You must now show delight; you must not show anger. You must not show upset, triumph, annoyance, rage or glee. Any emotion you present to us will be lapped up, even the smallest glint of delight in your eyes or a gesture such as giving us the middle finger. It is this failure to adhere to the Core Principle that results in so many failed attempts to secure revenge over my kind and me. Once you start giving us the attention when it is infused with emotion the balance of power shifts to us. Most victims have no awareness of this Core Principle and plough on wondering why they are not getting anywhere. They are bewildered, as we stand there smiling as you launch into a tirade before we join in, provoking you further. The application of the Core Principle is key to ensuring that your revenge campaign is effective.

Remember, your goal is to starve us of fuel. No Contact has done this and forced us to go elsewhere. If we interact with you during the revenge campaign the in those moments the only source, we can gather fuel from is you. If you are not providing it to us, then you begin to weaken us as I have described above. Once you begin to make us weak your activities will have greater effect on stripping us of what is central to us (I expand on this in later chapters). If you give us any fuel, then we become stronger again and we are equipped to fight back. You have to turn off the fuel as you apply your revenge campaign. This will start to have a paralytic effect so that we are at your mercy. How satisfying (though don't show it) would that be? Think of all the times you were paralysed with terror as we unleashed another awful manipulative and abusive act from our Devil's Toolkit. Recall the fear you felt when that happened. Now it is time to pay us back. With interest.

We know that because you are an empathic individual that emotions play a significant part in your life. You regard the expression of emotion as an important thing. You are also a devotee of love and therefore have a great belief in those emotions, which are associated with love - happiness, affection, caring, tenderness and the like. By contrast, dark and negative emotions are not things, which you prefer to address or associate with and that are why it is all the more satisfying when we are able to provoke these reactions in you. You are an emotional person. There is nothing wrong in that. In fact, we value this capacity for emotions that you have. This is one of the reasons why we select you are a victim, your capability to generate so much emotional content. Consider the times when your narcissist deployed the devaluation against you. You will remember a whole host of manipulative techniques, which were designed to control, provoke, browbeat and extract that prized negative emotional reactions as fuel. The times you curled up in a ball crying, the times you screamed as crockery was hurled about the room, the occasions when you shouted back frustration overloading you at the abhorrent, unjustified and quite frankly illogical treatment you were receiving. You may recall that the ways we treated you, which had the greatest impact upon you, were ones where we acted in a manner devoid of emotion. The cold, hard stares, which stunned you into submission. The savage comments that were delivered in a deadpan fashion. The way we would withdraw from providing you with affection, warmth, love or sex and instead behave like some cold automaton instead. Most of all, one of our most powerful manipulative techniques of course was subjecting you to the silent treatment. Whether it was remaining in your presence but ignoring you or absenting ourselves, this emotion free tool of manipulation always had a dramatic and devastating effect on you. Our acts and words that were so devoid of emotions cut you to the core. Now you are going to reverse that behaviour and apply it to us. This will wrong foot us. We expect you to behave in an emotional manner. We want you to and we need you to. By acting free of emotion you not only remove our fuel but you are also providing us with a stark reminder of who we really are, not what we think we are and that is not something we can countenance.

When we undertook our devaluation of you, you began to see us in our natural state. An individual devoid of compassion, warmth, love or affection. Somebody who can mimic all of those emotions but who is entirely incapable of feeling them. We have not been blessed with those emotions which you have and which you prize and treasure. The ability to be empathic, the capacity to love and care. The ability to be sympathetic and place yourself in the position of another. Remorse, guilt, accountability, regret and responsibility are not concepts applicable to us.

Yes, we have watched and studied so we can fool many people at the outset that we can produce such emotions but the reality is we cannot. Our emotional spectrum is extremely limited. This is part of our design because all those emotions, which you can experience, are denied to us because they serve no purpose to us. They will either prove of no use or in fact would hinder us from getting fuel and therefore we have never developed those emotions. In the same way that evolution supports survival of the fittest, we have developed to survive by harvesting fuel and becoming something, which is primed and created to do so to an optimum level. All those emotions, which get in the way of our stated mission, have never been granted to us. They serve no purpose. Instead we have only been allowed to experience truly other emotions which are there to allow us to carry out our one function and that is to obtain fuel. Accordingly, we are structured to feel rage, fury, envy, pride, arrogance, superiority, hatred, antipathy, omnipotence, boastfulness and jealousy. Those are the emotions that we have been granted. Each of those powers us forward in our pursuit of fuel. It is those emotions, which show what we truly are. We will repeatedly mask them because we are astute enough to know that their repeated application and airing is not deemed to be socially acceptable. We keep them under wraps and only call on them when it is required or when we can give full reign to them as we devalue you. It is this set of emotions which forms the basis for your targets in your revenge campaign. These emotions are what we are and you will focus your campaign against them, as I will detail below.

All of the acts, which you may take against us, must be administered in accordance with the Core Principle. Every time you consider what you might do to attack us, frustrate us and advance your campaign you must look at it with the gloss of the Core Principle applied to it. Remove the emotion. Do not use emotive words, do not engage in emotive gestures and do not show any emotion of any kind. The moment you do you are fuelling us and you start to lose. Keep in mind the need to appear neutral. Your words may be scathing but they must be delivered in a measured manner. They must not be shouted or yelled. You must avoid gesticulation or exaggerated movements, which would betray you as angry, irritated or anxious. Your expression should be open and neutral. It will take time to ensure that you always remember to apply this Core Principle but like anything, the more you apply it the easier it will become until acting in accordance with it will become second nature to you. It will take practice and it will take training but it is the central plank of a successful revenge campaign. Maintain this and you will not diminish the effect of the other acts that you will need to take in order to secure your revenge. Keep the Core Principle applied and you will not run the risk of granting power to the narcissist. Instead, you will maintain control and this in itself will cause us consternation. We are always used to having control. We control other people; the environment we operate in and most of all we control you.

When our hegemonic control is challenged we do not like it and if we find that we are struggling to assert it, this will weaken us further. The application of the Core Principle is essential to you achieving a successful revenge campaign and it will also provide you with a number of benefits as you are doing this.

Be aware that the application of the Core Principle will not achieve revenge. It will deprive us of fuel but if all your campaign consists of is not showing any emotion to us we will eventually seek our fuel elsewhere. You will have forced us to move on (until a Hoover occurs) but this is not revenge. Revenge goes far further than just not exhibiting emotion in front of us. I had this situation happen with an ex-girlfriend of mine called Kay. Kay applied the Core Principle and she was succeeding in draining my fuel through her cessation of its provision and moreover by her repeated criticism of me, as I shall now explain.

Kay was a flame-haired, freckled, brown-eyed sports enthusiast. She loved most sports so of course I did as well. We joined a local running club together and it was a running joke between us that each week we took it turns to chase after the other. After a number of failed attempts to escape my clutches it was evident that Kay had received some third party advice because her approach altered and it was evident that someone had schooled her in the art of No Contact. I found I was unable to reach her by telephone as she had evidently changed her mobile telephone number. That prevented me from sending text messages to her too. My e-mails bounced back as either I was blocked or the e-mail account she used had been closed. She had no landline at home and my attempts to contact her at work were being blocked by a gatekeeper who even I would have been proud of. I knew however that Kay could not avoid me forever. She had to interact with me because: -

1. I knew where she lived;

2. I knew where she worked;

3. I knew which gym she frequented; and

4. I knew she would keep attending the running club.

After my failed attempts to contact her through technology I pondered my next move. I was tempted to attend on her house and provoke her into speaking with me but there was a meeting of the running club coming up in a couple of days and I relished the opportunity of seeing how she would maintain No Contact with me. I had no concerns about her absenting herself from the club. She was too stubborn to do so and that would mean she was sacrificing something she enjoyed to avoid me. This of course is required if No Contact is to be implemented effectively but it was a mistake that Kay would make, or so I thought.

On the Tuesday evening I turned up at the running club and busied myself talking to a couple of female members who I knew and who I could tell were interested in me. This mild flirtation provided me with a useful burst of fuel as out of the corner of my eye I saw Kay walk onto the track. Immediately I felt the urge to walk over to her and speak to her. Her appearance had ignited my fury since she had criticised me by deciding to end our relationship but I could not lash out, not in front of the various members of the running club who had a high regard for me. It took considerable will power to fight down this urge, as I wanted to provoke her and generate a reaction as a precursor to hoovering her back in. I turned and smiled at her. She caught my eye but gave no reaction. I was not perturbed and was more amused and this only served to increase my desire to establish contact. The evening's session would commence with five warm up laps of the athletics track. This was done at a medium pace and therefore lent itself to being able to converse. I watched as Kay set off and I was pleased to see that she had not begun this warm-up with anyone by her side. I recognised that this was because the other members knew we always ran side-by-side during the warm-up and I saw no reason for this to change. I set off and soon caught her up, pulling alongside her. A couple of men ran just behind us and I could hear them talking about their respective days at work.

"Hello Kay," I said pleasantly, "what a pleasant surprise to see you, you seem to have gone missing. I have been worried about you."

She did not reply but continued to run, her eyes fixed on the track ahead.

"Have you been unwell?" I asked feigning concern.

She did not answer.

"Sudden trip away to Mars perhaps?" I remarked sarcastically. I noticed she increased her pace seeking to move away from me but it was easy enough to keep pace.

"Kidnapped and ransomed instead then?" I asked.

Still her silence was maintained. Her face was expressionless. I could feel my fury igniting again as she continued to ignore me. How dare she do that to me? The pack of runners was around me and though I wanted to shout at her and call her an ungrateful whore and a gold-digging slut the maintenance of the façade took preference to such an outburst of fury. Whoever was schooling her knew their stuff.

"Oh I see; some silent treatment is it? My, such hypocrisy after all the times you called me for doing so to you. I did not have you down as hypocrite Kay but I guess I am just going to have to add it to the other names I have for you aren't I?" I said as I ran next to her my voice low and menacing. Still she maintained that implacable visage as we circled the track.

"Bitch. That is one name for you. Slut. There is another. Ungrateful cow. I have helped you so much, helped you with this, your running and this is how you repay me? Walking away and cutting off contact with me. Jesus you take the biscuit after all the badgering you did for me to join this club," I hissed as we ran but her neutral expression did not change. I continued to hiss insults at her but they were just bouncing off.

"Oh and the sponsorship too. I fucking got my firm to sponsor your annual dinner. That wasn't easy or cheap was it, but I still did it for you and this is the thanks I get. Well you can shove that sponsorship up your backside you fucking bitch because tomorrow it gets cancelled," I threatened.

Her eyes switched to me and her mouth opened. A reaction? No, she caught herself and closed her mouth and turned her eyes back to staring straight ahead. This encouraged me but I was getting nothing from her. No reaction and no fuel. I wanted to lash out and shout and yell at her but I was being prevented from doing so and her ignoring me was wounding me. I could feel the sharp pain burning through me at this criticism of me and I had to channel my power to address the injury and shield myself. I needed to get a reaction from her. I kept issuing threats about ruining the running club but her expression did not change, she just started to speed up and I with her as well until we were both running clear of the pack. My insults continued but I was not able to break through this stony expression. There was no irritation, no upset, and no anger; there was nothing. I could feel my control crumbling, as the ignited fury being used to shield wanted instead to be directed in a white-hot burst against Kay in order to punish her. In order to provoke. In order to gain fuel. If I lacked the discipline and awareness of my lower-functioning brethren that burst of fury would have erupted but I was just about managing to keep it under control. I knew however with her repeated criticisms by way of ignoring me that I could not maintain this situation for long. We were now on the other side of the track, away from the main pack and no doubt they were wondering why we have surged ahead. The thought that they may be impressed with our display of athleticism provided me a degree of fuel but it was only small and was being eaten up by trying to deal with these ongoing criticisms. A handful of field athletes were limbering up in the area encircled by the track but we were away from close scrutiny and it was then that I knew what to do. I released another barrage of insults and threats and still she maintained her implacable expression. She accelerated away and I knew I had to act. I kicked on and followed suit as I pulled alongside her and then applied my spikes to the side of her left calf. If anybody happened to see it happen it would have looked like an accident as I overtook her. I heard her gasp and then there was the noise of her hitting the track. I continued running as if I had noticed then looked over my shoulder to see her sat on the track, hand gripping the injury.

"Got you," I muttered and jogged to where she was.

I bent down and the look of pain on her face and the blood trickling down her leg immediately gave me that burst of fuel that I needed.

"Get away from me," she said and put up her hand. Good, more fuel.

"Let me look," I declared feigning concern as I pulled her hand away.

"That will need cleaning up," I remarked.

"I said get away from me you vile bastard, I do not want anything to do with you anymore, stay away from me," she said between pursed lips but the anger in her eyes had shattered her neutral stance and the fuel was no flowing my way.

"We had better get you into the clubhouse," I said loudly as other members of the club caught up with us. I saw Kay look at them with a degree of nervousness and knew she would not push me away in front of them.

"Saul, will you give me a hand with Kay please?" I asked one of the men nearby. He nodded as we slipped an arm about our shoulders each.

"There is no need I can get there myself," said Kay.

"Nonsense," I overrode, "nasty spiking you got there, must have caught you as I went past you."

"Yes, that will need a bandage," commented Saul.

We helped her off the track and began to head for the clubhouse. Another member drew alongside Saul and began speaking to him as I turned to Kay who was trying to maintain her composure but her eyes were welling with tears. Whether they were tears of pain or of frustration I was not entirely sure.

"Nice try Kay, you were doing quite well for a while there but you don't ignore me, ever, do you understand?" I hissed in her ear as I gripped her wrist hard with my hand. She winced and the tears increased and more fuel came my way. I waited and then she gave a nod of resignation. It was almost imperceptible but not to me, not when I knew what to look for.

Thus Kay, with evidently some outside help had sought to instigate No Contact and was doing so effectively until she made the error of coming to the running club. Her obstinate refusal to sacrifice her love of running, even for a few weeks, paved the way for her No Contact failing. If I had attended the club and she had not done so for several weeks, I would have stopped going and tried to approach her at home or at work. I only attended the club to mirror her in the first place. By turning up she sailed too close to my orbit and although her disciplined display of ignoring me and applying the Core Principle was almost admirable it failed. It pains me to admit that she almost had the upper hand and I would had to have broken off and turned to a supplementary source, most likely the two female athletes I mentioned at the beginning of this recollection, to gain fuel to repair the wounds she had inflicted from her criticisms through ignoring me. She almost succeeded in winning the first battle and forcing a retreat. This shows the power of the Core Principle and also how when used in tandem with the very thing that wounds us, criticism it becomes an effective tool. It would have been far more effective if she had known precisely what to target but it was clear her tutor was not aware of that and that is something that will be discussed in more detail below.

Accordingly, by keeping emotion out of all your interaction with us, you will be able to focus on what needs to be done in order to secure revenge. What then is the ultimate aim of this revenge campaign? This is what we turn to next.

3. The Ultimate Aim

What is the ultimate aim of the revenge campaign? You may think that it is achieving freedom from the narcissist that you became entangled with. There is no denying that this is indeed the aim of many people but this can be achieved through No Contact. If that is what you want to achieve then you have no need to embark on a revenge campaign. Is it perhaps a desire to make us see the error of our ways and commit to change? If that is your ultimate aim, you will have a long wait. Most of our kind (although admittedly not all) does see that what we do is considered as wrong by other people but that has no impact on us for the following reasons: -

1.   We are not fashioned to experience regret, compassion, guilt or remorse;

2.   We regard what we do as entirely necessary to serve our purposes;

3.   If there is collateral damage as a consequence of us achieving our aims then so be it.

We know what we do and we realise that you and many other label it as wrong but that is because you judge up by a certain set of criteria. We neither regard what we do as wrong and nor do we care because we must act this way in order to preserve ourselves. There may be times when we will admit what we do is wrong, apologise and offer some form of contrition. None of this is genuine but we know this is what you want to see and hear and therefore we use in order to extract further fuel from you and especially if we think that there is a risk that you may try and leave us. It is all a sham and again only designed to suit our purposes. Similarly, the prospect of us changing is nil. Why would we ever change when we excel at what we do? Our function is to gather fuel. We are fantastic at it and along the way we walk the earth like a god. We pick our subjects, draw them to us, convert minions to carry out our works and then treat people as we want. We answer to nobody. We go where we want and do as we please. Such a boundless existence is one, which we would not want to give up. Neither would you if you were in our shoes. We know you are good at putting yourself in someone else's position, so consider that if you were me and you could do as I have just described, knowing that this is what must be done to maintain your existence, would you not decide that change is not only impossible but undesirable? The honest answer is yes. Accordingly, if the ultimate aim of your revenge campaign is to bring about some sense of remorse and change in our behaviour then you are mistaken.

Perhaps instead then that the desire to achieve revenge has the ultimate aim of humiliating the narcissist? This gets closer to the mark. We cannot stand to be humiliated. This is in effect a criticism and undermines our greatness, erodes our brilliance and makes us too much like you. This will ignite our rage and cause us to go on the attack in order to address the wound that you have inflicted against us. This fury enables us to repair the wound and then continue to gather fuel. In all cases we achieve this. You may do something, which offends us mightily. Often you will not actually realise that it is that you have done but you will cause us grave offence by ignoring us, failing to acknowledge our greatness or drawing attention to you and away from us. This amounts to criticism. We are wounded and must respond in order to close the wound as soon as possible. Our ignited fury is used to this and you can understand more about this works in my book **Fury.** Once the ignited fury has addressed the wound in the relevant manner we will need more fuel since we have used this fuel to power our repairs of the wound and our shielding of our self during those repairs.

What then if you could keep wounding us? What might happen then? Our fury would keep igniting and we would face a choice. Do we go on the attack (if able to and circumstances allow), do we shield ourselves or do we withdraw? Those three options all allow us to repair the wound you have caused. What if after one wound there is another and then another? Our responses remain the same and we will fight to repair those wounds. Each time we are forced to do so however we are using up our fuel, the fuel that maintains our construct. Thus a concerted attack of criticism and one from which we cannot withdraw will force us to attack back or shield and keep using up fuel. What if the availability of fuel has become diminished? What if you have applied No Contact to deprive us of fuel and then have delivered certain acts as part of the revenge campaign applying the Core Principle so those acts cannot and do not provide us with any fuel? Such a situation could be likened to us being curled up in a ball, unable to crawl away as you stand over us raining blow after blow upon us and weakening us further.

The removal of fuel will increase our vulnerability. The repeated criticisms delivered in tandem with the Core Principle will ignite our fury and thus deplete our existing stores of fuel. If these criticisms are maintained and we cannot find fresh fuel, we use up what we have defending ourselves from the criticisms until it is gone. At this point we are left with nothing to keep the construct together. The shards, sections, pieces and fragments that we have taken from others to create that which we want the world to know us as can no longer remain in place. As they fall then the prison we have constructed is breached and that wretched creature will come forth and what we thought we were and what we wanted the world to regard us as is consigned to oblivion and we are destroyed.

I can tell you that even as I write about such a prospect a feeling of unease has wrapped around me. It is not something I like to contemplate but I know that this is how you will achieve the ultimate aim of your revenge campaign. The ultimate aim is the destruction of the narcissist. Gone is the grandiose, entitled, boastful, charismatic champion. He has had his cloak stripped away from him by these concerted criticisms and the crippling effects of the cessation of fuel. The edifice that once existed and strode the world, dominating and impressing has vanished. The brilliance has evaporated, the magnificence has disappeared and the impressive has become the pathetic. We want the world to see us as the champions that we want to be. We survive for so long by conning those around us into believing that that is what we truly are. Many people cannot see through the illusion and accept it their whole lives. They cannot be criticised for doing so because that is what we want them to believe and we work damn hard to achieve it through the construction of our illusion and the unleashing of all our manipulative wiles. Those people are like the majority of the people in the Matrix films. They are unaware of the reality and are perfectly content to remain ensconced in the illusion because it suits them just as much as it suits us. They are blind but it does not matter to them. Those people are often our minions and even when they are not they are perfectly content to remain as by-standers gawping open-mouthed at our brilliance, accepting it and never challenging it. By shattering the illusion through your revenge campaign you will be doing so in a way that lays us bare and destroys us. This methodology is such that we will not be able to use our usual tactic of labelling you as crazy and a trouble maker to all and sundry because you will have not only tipped the balance of control in your favour but you will be applying the Core Principle.

It is an acknowledged fact that when we discard you, your immediate reaction is to want to tell everyone how badly you have been treated and what a terrible person I am. This rarely works for you. Yes, there may be one or two of your most loyal supporters who will believe you but the majority of those we have engaged with will not believe you. This is because we will have done such a good job of maintaining the façade that your wild protestations of abuse and terrible treatment will just not sit right with what these people know of us. We will have decided when we were going to discard you and thus ahead of this act we will have spent our time engaging in a smear campaign and a character assassination. The charm offensive will have been planted deep in the minds of all those we have influenced and remember we are the masters of charm. Not only have we convinced them of our balance, our attempts to help you and our overall decency we will have been explaining to them ho you are unhinged, that you need help and that you have been the one who has acted without rhyme or reason. You have abused us despite our best endeavours to help. Your situation is not helped that by the time this happens you will be at low ebb. You will feel exhausted, drained and battered. All of your resources will be at a low point and your frustration at us having outflanked you once again will result in you engaging in behaviour, which only underlines what we have said about you. You will be wide-eyed, hysterical and tearful. A complete contrast to the controlled and smooth approach we adopted. You will shout, plead and find yourself tied up in knots. Most normal people do not like conflict. They do not like disruption and contention. You will appear as the one kicking up trouble and therefore you will be branded as the crazy one. This tactic on our part is so effective at keeping you pouring fuel our way whilst gathering sympathy (and yet more fuel) from all the spectators to the drama. Thus you become weaker and we become stronger. We are able to move onto our new primary source of fuel as the supplementary sources pump fuel our furiously in our favour. You meanwhile are left sprawled in the dust until such time as we return to pick over you again and extract more fuel from a Hoover.

By following the Core Principle in pursuit of this ultimate aim this defence mechanism will be denied to us. You have remained devoid of emotion, measured and levelheaded and those who are the spectators can see this. Even if you do not have the support of others to the degree that you will like, by adopting the Core Principle you will put yourself in a position of strength as your actions are governed by reason rather than the knee jerk emotional responses we look to evoke from you.

Accordingly, you will be looking to strike us down by launching criticisms at us. These will wound. I have explained to you how you must approach this revenge campaign by adopting the Core Principle. I have explained to you also what your ultimate aim is and how this can be achieved through the cessation of fuel combined with the repeated delivery of criticisms. You then need to know and understand where these criticisms must be aimed for them to have maximum effectiveness. It is all very well having the state-of-the-art weaponry but if you aim it at the wrong place you will still not defeat your opponent. Thus we turn our attention to the question of identifying your targets as you seek the ultimate aim in your revenge campaign.

4. Identifying Your Targets

In determining what your targets are we should first consider how the narcissist lands blows against you. I do not normally like to let you have the spotlight shine on you but for the purposes of conveying how your revenge campaign needs to be carried out, you are going to be centre stage. Just for a short while anyway. When we devalue you, you are subjected to emotional, physical, financial and sexual abuse. Sometimes all of these forms of abuse, sometimes only some of them dependent on the type of narcissist you have become involved with. Those are the methods by which we attack you, but what is it about you that we target for maximum effect. Keep in mind that we have spent time targeting you and ensuring that you meet our criteria so you become an ideal appliance for us. Not only does this mean that we need to satisfy ourselves that you provide us with plenty of high-grade value, we want to be sure that you will adhere to the other empathic behaviours such as wanting it fix us, clinging on to the golden period, needing to know and such like. These traits and others beside are what go into your make-up which makes you desirable to us whether you are an empathic person, a super empathic individual or a co-dependent. You can read more about how this targeting is done in a forthcoming book **Sitting Target How the Narcissist Chooses You** but for the purposes of your revenge campaign it is enough to know that we spend time and energy ensuring you fit with the model of empathic compliance that we require. We watch you; we research you and your life and when we engage with you we move quickly to establish that you are of the calibre. Once that has been achieved then the seduction begins. Since we are experts in the art of observation and ascertaining precisely what it is about you that serves our purpose, then we are equally capable at knowing precisely what to target in you to have maximum effect when we devalue, discard and Hoover you. We know from our preparatory work the very things that are central to your existence. We identify and recognise that certain traits run through your core and that an assault on these central ideals will not only yield massive amounts of fuel during devaluation but they will bring you to your knees so you can be flung aside. Horrible? Yes. Cynical? Of course we are. Necessary. Absolutely. Accordingly, when we commence our devaluation of you, the abusive manipulative tools that we deploy will be focussed on the following of your attributes: -

1.   Self-esteem;

2.   Capacity to comprehend;

3.   `Critical thinking and evaluation;

4.   Sense of empathy;

5.   Capability to care;

6.   Desire to understand;

7.   Devotion to the concept of love;

8.   Belief in inner goodness

9.   Delivery of truth

You may have red hair, be good at tennis and have a shapely bottom. You may be an excellent cook, have a keen interest in English Stuart history and be able to strip down a car engine. It might be the case that you are a bookworm with an extensive knowledge of classical writings. You may be a film buff or a connoisseur of fine wines. There will be a whole array of traits that you will have but all of these are just the gloss on who you are as an empathic individual. Yes, those traits will have interested us but purely for the purpose of mirroring them back at you when we seduced you. You may think that your support for a particular charity, which has gone on for twenty-five years is very much a part of you but it is not. It is not part of your central core of qualities. All of these interests, hobbies and abilities are superficial in nature. Certainly we will look to spoil and denigrate them during our devaluation of you but they are not what truly make you. It is those items above (or ones of a similar nature), which make you who you are. It is those central qualities that we will unleash our devaluation against, as our love bombs turn into barbed and crushing weapons which tear chunks from you. We know what you are. We know because we need to know in order to effect our own existence and maintain the same. We have been furnished with the knowledge and insight into what you are so that when the time comes we can look to crush those absolutely crucial qualities and thus draw more fuel as you lie twitching and broken before us. We will rarely deliver the coup de grace, as we will allow you to crawl away and replenish your fuel levels in readiness for our Hoovering of you. Keep that fact in mind. We will not put you out of your misery. We will not end it. We will not show some compassion (we do not feel it) after everything that you have endured by ending it with one swift, executory strike. Remember that when you are conducting your critical assaults against us. We spared you and left you writhing in agony. You will not do the same.

You may be thinking at this point that the revenge campaign sounds too brutal for you. You are not comfortable with the concept of hurting someone else irrespective of the harm they have caused you. You may feel that engaging in such behaviours has you sailing close to being like us rather than the empathic person you are. If such thoughts are dominating your mind set, then revenge is not for you. However much you may think that you want to achieve it, if you are thinking these thoughts, that you feel it is cruel no matter how deserved it might be, then you should re-consider whether a revenge campaign is something you are cut out for. Drawing a line at No Contact and maintaining that and moving on accordingly will better serve you. Revenge is not for you.

If on the other hand you realise that what you have been put through requires addressing and that you require closure by achieving the ultimate aim and destroying your narcissist, then a revenge campaign is what you require.

Thus you can see we know exactly what it is about your make-up that can be attacked and thus will bring about your near destruction. By targeting those traits and attributes that I have described above we are landing fearsome and terrible blows against you. By way of example when we gas light you, blame shift and triangulate you this is all designed to wear down your critical thinking. In tandem with the exhaustion that you are feeling, the sense of a warped reality where you become unsure of what is right and what has been said or done erodes you critical thinking. This enables us to keep you in a state of paralysis, as you are unable to process what we are doing to you in an effective way and thus you remain where you are. You once prided yourself on your ability to evaluate situations and especially ones where emotions and feelings are involved. By attacking this trait of yours then we are stripping, mauling and denting a central element of your character. This will not only leave you exposed to further injurious intent but will mean that you are being beaten down. We will assault most if not all of those traits listed above in a variety of different ways. Some are overt and others most subtle, but their combined effect is to damage those key traits of yours until you are only worth discarding.

Accordingly, in order to land your criticisms in the most effective places, so that they can cause the maximum damage you need to know what our central character attributes are. These are what are referred to as the Narcissistic Pillars. You need to know what these pillars are and then you need to understand the best way of attacking them so they topple to the ground. Attacking these pillars is the most effective way of achieving the ultimate aim. By bringing these pillars crashing to the ground you will then cause such massive criticisms, which when combined with a fuel shortage, we will not be able to recover from.

Part of the skill of identifying these pillars lies in finding them amidst all of the illusory segments, pieces and shards that we have accumulated as we have stolen from those around us and cloaked them in those things we want for ourselves and for the world to see. Excellence at sport, a proficient public speaker, the life and soul of the party, a formidable orator, a sexual Olympian and so much more. These elements we find in others and using the fuel powered magnetism of the construct we strip them away and take them for ourselves and pass them off as what we really are. This is what we really want to be. This is what we want you and the world to regard us as. Successful, charismatic, charitable, decent, good-looking, engaging, alluring, achieving and so on. Yet it is not these stolen attributes that you should be sharpening your criticisms for. They are just part of the illusion and if you pull those shards away the damage will be minimal and all we will do is replace them from somewhere else. No sooner have you removed on piece then we will have acquired two more. You will try and wrench away other pieces but your criticisms although wounding will not do enough damage and thus we will be in a position to either attack you or shield ourselves and repair. This is an elementary error, which many people make when they try to strike us down, that and continue to provide us with fuel. Adopting either stance means that your revenge campaign will be doomed for failure. It is perhaps appropriate at this juncture to provide you with an example of how attacking our illusion will only result in failure.

For this we turn to an ex-girlfriend named Joanne. Keen readers may recall that she always had to touch me. Joanne began as a decent appliance. Her need to touch meant that she started out flowing with fuel through her every gesture. A gentle hand on the shoulder, a tickle of the ribs, a hand running through my hair and shortly thereafter two hands cupping my face as she whispered to me how much she loved me. She showed promise but alas she, like so many others, let me down and the fuel began to flow less and without the customary strength that I had become used to. Consequently, the devaluation began as I sought out the negative fuel, which was so necessary for me and it was not long before I reached into my devil's toolkit and commenced my manipulations. She was completely flummoxed when her very touch made me shrink back in disgust. Her eyes filled with tears as I moved away and snapped at her to stop touching me. The hurt oozed from her and with it the fuel. She evidently did not listen as she kept trying to hug me, to rub my back, caress me, touch me, brush against me and hold me. With each attempt my irritation grew and I would bark at her to get out of my space. Her confusion was tangible. I had gone from someone who revelled in her tactile approach to someone who regarded her as having a leper's touch. Yet she still kept pressing to touch me, to subsume me within her hugs and I took to grabbing her wrists as those hands snaked towards me and wrenching her arms downwards with a firm admonishment.

I forget how long this devaluation continued as I now had Karen the caretaker in my sights. Kind, caring Karen whose cool hands would sooth my fevered brow as I told her about the obsessive Joanne who would not leave me alone despite my many attempts to escape her. Karen, like all of them, fell for the crazy ex routine and sought to ease my concerns with her tender ministrations. How I preferred her elegant touch to that of the ham-fisted Joanne. The fuel now flowed from Karen and was of a far superior quality to anything Joanne ever provided to me. I knew I had made the correct choice. As I always did. Joanne had served her purpose and it was time to jettison her. On this occasion I decided that silent treatment would be best and I rejected her calls, removed her from my social media and informed my secretary that she was not put any calls through from her. She tried to be clever and called using different names but my ever loyal secretary, who is in love with me, did not recognise those names but did recognise Joanne's voice so she was unable to get past my gatekeeper. She is most dependable is Sally but that is what comes from always giving her the hope that one day I might just take her on a date.

Joanne then went quiet and I was enjoying the golden period with the wonderful Karen with no need to Hoover Joanne just yet such was the premium quality of fuel being supplied by Karen. I recall it was late September and was a pleasant autumnal morning when I and some business contacts, which were all sucking my kneecaps in the hope of winning business from me, were gathered on the golf course. It was the fourth tee as this was the one, which was nearest the road, which wound through the countryside where the gold course was situated. I was holding forth before teeing off, impressing the other three men who were playing golf with me when I saw from the corner of my eye Joanne's car. He drove a lime green VW Beetle and subtle it was not. Her car drew to a halt by the edge of the golf course as I delayed my shot and watched as she clambered out and hopped over the fence and began striding purposefully across the fairway towards us.

"Looks like we have a visitor, has she come to caddy for you HG?" joked one of the men.

"If she has she is running rather late. Good God, do you know who it is chaps? It is this mad woman who has been stalking me. I once spoke to her in a bar and she is obsessed with me. Keeps waiting for me outside the office and rings up every day. Absolutely barking mad. You might want to keep a five iron handy in case she gets over excited," I laughed as Joanne approached.

"Seriously?" remarked one of the men and I nodded.

"Do you want me to get rid of her?" asked another.

"No, no, let's hear what the crazy cow has to say, this will give us something to laugh about back at the club house," I remarked entirely relaxed.

Joanne arrived and stood before and beneath us. We were on the elevated tee and arranged so that it would have been awkward for her to stand on it also so she had to stand at a disadvantage from the beginning.

"Can I help you? This is private property," I said firmly.

"What's going on? I have been trying to contact you for weeks. You just vanished."

I turned to the other golfers.

"See? I told you, won't leave me alone."

"Leave you alone? Why should I when you just drop me without any explanation whatsoever," she shouted at me, eyes blazing with anger.

"I have no idea what you are talking about but you really ought to leave. The green keeper won't take kindly to you stomping across his fairway."

"What do you mean you have no idea what I am talking about? I have been in a relationship with you for a year although God knows why after the way you have been treating me."

"I am not sure what goes on in side that head of yours miss but we have not been in a relationship at all."

"What?" she exploded. "Well how come I know, how come I know, "she repeated, "that you drive a BMW 5-series a black one."

"Because you stand outside my office and see me get in it."

"Look love, just piss off out of the way will you, we are trying to play golf?" interjected one of my companions.

"No I will not," shouted Joanne her face red with frustration and anger. "Do you know who you are playing with? This man is a fraud. He is a cheat and a liar and he has made my life hell," her voice broke as she fought to keep her relative composure. I stood there entirely calm drinking in this fuel and shook my head.

"You know he cheats at golf, he does, he will make down too low a score, he told me he does it every time he plays because he has to win," she said jabbing a forefinger at the score card held by one of the men.

"Have you finished?" I asked.

"Oh he doesn't like to lose does HG? Oh not at all and he won't want to lose face in front of all of you either. Don't believe a word he says, he would not know the truth if it hit him in the face. He lies all the time."

"All right love, you need to clear off you've said your piece now fuck off," remonstrated another of my companions. One stepped forward as if to remove her but I raised my hand to halt him. I let her continue as she danced from one leg to the other as she sought to embarrass me. She tried to convince the men that she knew me by trotting out private information about me but each time I just commented that how she knew this from following me, standing outside my house, harassing my family and even stealing my post from a post man. I knew because my companions wanted my favour and they admired who I was that they would not believe a word she said so I was entirely content for her to rant as it provided me with fuel.

I knew what she was trying to do. She was trying to embarrass me by attacking me in front of fellow businessmen and also lambasting my preference for playing golf. I knew she thought that if she challenged me here in front of people I would do anything to shut her up and that I would agree to sit down with her later and discuss things. I had her sized up all right. As soon as I had seen her leave the car I knew what she would be trying to do. She was trying to attack part of what I was in the hope of dismantling it. She wanted to rip away that shard that related to my golf. She wanted to smash the section, which showed my business acumen. She wanted to tear down the fragment concerned with my standing in front of these three men but I was too strong for her and of course she made the fundamental error of doing all this whilst angry and upset. I let her continue with her ill-fated attack as the fuel flowed until one of my companions clearly irritated that he was being kept from his game and the nineteenth hole stepped forward and grabbed her, placing her over his shoulder. "Right missy, time you left," he roared as he began to advance back across the fairway as Joanne yelled and protested her hands beating his back. We roared with delight as he paced away.

"Watch out John, she might get attached to you now and think you are an item," I shouted to his departing figure. We watched as John shoved her into her car and stood waiting for her to drive off. He pulled out his phone as if threatening to call someone; probably the police and we saw her pull away and speed off down the road.

"What a lunatic, you need to get an order or something keeping her away," commented Paul.

"Oh she is harmless, just utterly deranged, I seem to attract them," I remarked as I began my practice swing.

Joanne's attack failed. She sought to attack things important to me but she targeted the wrong things and she did so whilst pouring with emotion, which only served to provide me with fuel. Trying to upbraid me in such a way only made her look stupid and played right into my hands as to the type of stalking fruitcake I had painted her out to be. She made three further attempts all again aimed at embarrassing me. Outside my house in front of my neighbours, at a restaurant when I was with Karen having clearly followed us and once when she bumped into Karen and I when we were out shopping. The final time perturbed Karen and I made arrangements for a couple of lieutenants to pay Joanne a visit. Her pathetic and failed campaign to try and seek revenge against me halted after that. Every time she had presented in an emotional manner, unable to keep her obvious distress and anger under control. This gave me fuel so that her name-calling and piss poor attempts to embarrass me and strip away elements of my creation failed. I was too powerful for her and easily able to deal with her for she was unable to land a blow. Her criticism was wrapped up in emotion and it was like trying to stab me with a knife, which had been shrouded in a blanket. Accordingly, trying to attack me in such a way will always fail. You are giving me fuel and you are attacking the wrong targets. The result can only be failure.

In the same way that we attack the central traits, which create your core in order to maximise our extraction of fuel and devaluation of you, you must target your criticism of us by attacking out central traits. What are they? Remember, you are not looking to attack those characteristics which we have stolen form other people because they are not us. They are not our beliefs. All you will be doing is removing a projection but failing to land any effective blows against us. We are not people who have been furnished with empathy like you. We experience a form of happiness but it is not a central trait. It is linked to the accumulation and wielding of power. There are many traits, which you have that we do not. There are also those traits, which normal people have which we have not been provided with. I am sure you can list many of them yourself. What you need to focus on is identifying and understanding what the central core characteristics are that appertain to the narcissist. How they govern his or her existence and in turn realising that these are your targets. These central core characteristics are our Narcissistic Pillars. Know what they are, understand them and target them. Do so applying the Core Principle and you will then be able to achieve the ultimate aim.

What then are those Narcissistic Pillars? What are those traits that we possess which are used to dominate and subjugate but once identified and targeted make us vulnerable to our destruction? There are eight in total. The elite greater narcissist will have all eight and thus you face a considerable challenge in toppling all of those pillars in order to secure the ultimate aim and your revenge. Lesser narcissists and especially those of the victim variety will have fewer of these pillars. Accordingly, before I reveal to you what the eight narcissistic pillars are it will be appropriate to consider what type of narcissist you are dealing with.

5. Identifying Your Narcissist

The classification of the type of narcissist that you have become entangled with is dependent on their level of functioning, desire to crush you, fixation with the mind and dedication to the body. The level of functioning will apply to considerations of mind and also the body. I am familiar with these classes of narcissist through my observation of my kind and interaction with those that form part of my family and background. In considering how to identify your narcissist you need to have regard to the two categories from which they may be drawn.

Firstly, there are the relevant schools. This covers the Lesser, Mid-Range or Greater Narcissist. Then there are secondly the cadres, which are applicable to the Victim, Somatic, Cerebral and Elite Narcissists. A narcissist is drawn from both a school and a cadre but there are some combinations, which cannot be achieved, as they are mutually opposite.

The Schools

The Lesser Narcissist

The Lesser Narcissist is typically low functioning. He is unlikely to know what he is and will reject any suggestion that he is a narcissist, instead retreating into blame shifting and projection. The Lesser Narcissist has just as great a need for fuel as any other narcissist but will always take the path of least resistance to obtain this fuel. The Hoover from a Lesser Narcissist will neither be intense nor will it be sustained once he recognises that he is facing considerable resistance. He will instead seek out a new primary source of fuel instead as this will be easier. He has no desire to seek near annihilation of his victims and instead once discarded only Hoover should they present the opportunity on a plate for him to do so. The Lesser Narcissist has lower energy levels and is very much a creature of economy. He sees little to be gained in higher stake approaches even if the promise of the fuel should such an approach succeed be fantastic. He would rather find an easier route. It is not the case that he or she is not a risk-taker but it turns on the fact that they cannot in fact be bothered to chase difficult (albeit more rewarding fuel) and will instead take it from easy sources. They classically always look for the low hanging fruit.

The Mid-Range Narcissist

The Mid-Range Narcissist possesses a reasonable level of functioning. He will work harder than a Lesser Narcissist to achieve his aims and will push harder when Hoovering but he lacks the superior attributes of the Greater Narcissist and does no share the malign intent that the Greater Narcissist is known for. The Mid-Range Narcissist will engage in sustained Hoovers and will look further a field than a Lesser Narcissist to do so. The Mid-Range Narcissist is usually identified by reason of omission. They do not exhibit the incandescent fury, malign intent and utter driven nature of the Greater Narcissist. By contrast they do not either show the economy of approach nor the lesser functioning ability of the Lesser Narcissist. Accordingly, if the narcissist that you have entangled with does not show any Lesser of Greater traits then you can safely place him or her as a Mid-Range Narcissist.

The Greater Narcissist

The Greater Narcissist (sometimes known as the malign narcissist) is a high functioning individual. This narcissist will be well aware of what he or she does, the nature of its impact yet has no regard for the chaos caused or the collateral damage generated. The Greater Narcissist can be identified by virtue of increased energy levels, the greater intensity of the Hoover, the sustaining of a longer period of Hoover and an all-pervading malevolence. The Greater Narcissist will look to crush his or her victim to near obliteration in the ruthless pursuit of punishment. The Lesser Narcissist has no interest in punishment. The Mid Range will achieve punishment if little effort is required. The Greater Narcissist has punishment very much on his or her agenda and will readily expend considerable energies in achieving this so long as sufficient fuel exists to support such a campaign. The Greater Narcissist has a more expansive manipulative toolkit and is capable of wreaking extensive harm to those who cross his or her path. A Greater Narcissist, if he so chooses, could readily seduce a Lesser Narcissist although naturally such a step would be fuel-limited and the categories of empathic individual, super empathic individual and co-dependent are vastly preferred.

Turning to the cadres. By way of reminder there are four. Victim, Cerebral, Somatic and Elite. We address the Victim Narcissist first.

Victim Narcissist

All narcissists play at being the victim at some point but not all narcissists are of the victim variety. Non-victim narcissists are content to use their perception of victim hood by virtue of manipulating their targets and victims. Furthermore, they will use their perception as being a victim for the purposes of driving their desire to act against people. Non-victim narcissists use the concept of being a victim as device and place it on themselves and remove it at will like a mask. True Victim Narcissists adopt a permanent state of being a victim both in outlook and behaviour. They regard the world as a place whereby they have been denied their rightful inheritance of looks, intellect, wealth and power and instead they rely on others to provide it to them instead. The Victim Narcissist will look to others to repair his failings such as lack of money, lack of home, lack of job and overall lack of competence. He will not look for his narcissism to be fixed because he is unaware of what he is since the Victim Narcissist is low functioning and can only be from the school of lesser narcissism.

Should you become entangled with a Victim Narcissist he or she may lash out at you. Indeed, owing to their low functioning, physical abuse ranks higher as a manipulative tool with these individuals. This lashing out however is not borne of a malign nature because the Victim Narcissist lacks both the capability and desire to behave in a malign way. You will not find a Victim Narcissist who is malign.

The Victim Variety of narcissist is somebody who lacks the body and looks obsession of the somatic narcissist and also lacks the intellect of the cerebral

49

narcissist. He is typically a low-functioning narcissist since he does not inherently have the wit or intelligence to seduce his victims through words and demonstrations of intellectual brilliance. Neither does he have the drive or discipline to take care of himself physically, dress well, and have a rigorous hygiene and looks maintenance ritual. He is however a narcissist and needs to seduce his victims all the same and he does so by presenting as a victim who needs looking after.

They also do not tend to love-bomb hugely effectively but instead they merely hide their savage side in the initial stages so they are at least not off-putting. I also tend to think that they draw their victims in not by a show of supremacy and strength but rather by eliciting sympathy. They play on the empath's sense of caring and nurturing and present as a victim in order to be mothered by the empath. Accordingly, they do not exhibit the same degree of allure, charisma and all around sparkling brilliance as we do. They are still able to draw people in because there are caregivers who do not care so much about how someone looks and so on, but feel sorry for them and want to care for them and make them better. Similarly, in sexual matters they exhibit no brilliance between the sheets and may even demonstrate incompetence in order to draw further sympathy and invite the caring empath to teach them to be better. These narcissists are entirely self-centred and lack the charm and tools to draw their victims in with brilliance and magnificence. These narcissists do tend to be from the lower functioning variety that is not especially good at anything. They will provide some embellishment but again because they are low- functioning they will lack the intelligence, guile and wit to conjure up fantastic tales of achievement and accomplishment. Instead, they need to keep their abusive streak in check, something they are able to do but they need to find some other way of drawing in their victims. They cannot hold up anything shiny or sparkling in the way that most of our kind does. Instead, they do the reverse. What they exhibit is rusting, battered and dented but they do it in a "Shucks look at me, I am in a bit of a mess, and I need someone to help me out, would that kind person be you?" They present their victim status very early on and this will not be attractive to many people but it will draw certain people to them, those who want to care for them, mother them and make them become better. The Victim Narcissist often lacks any financial resources, may not be employed (and if he or she is they will be in a low-skilled occupation) and will relish the opportunity to forgo working so that the victim can support them. This type of narcissist has no interest in status unlike say an Elite Narcissist, but instead their sense of entitlement will outweigh any concerns about status. You should look after them if you say you love them. They are entitled to be cared for by reason of the fact that they are victims. They will regard themselves as a bit of a rough diamond, which needs polishing up and the empathic victim they have selected is just the person to do this.

Since this type of narcissist does not rely on being a shining beacon of attraction to people but rather a battered old vehicle which needs some tender loving care he sees no reason to let the flattery flow. There is little in the way of grandiose gestures or extravagance. Instead he will just play the victim card repeatedly in order to keep that empath looking after him and drawn to him. He is appreciative of the attention and caring and why not? He is gaining fuel but is also being looked after. He will probably not work and rely on the financial ability of the victim in that respect. He will help a little, just enough to avoid reprimand and enough to draw thanks from the empath. He keeps the abuse in check and therefore whilst never over the top in word or gesture he is pleasant enough. He certainly is not horrible His gratitude at being looked after and given attention by the empath satisfies the empath and they are willing to overlook the deficiencies because they feel good about taking care of this person. Since this type of narcissist has no need to look good, sound great and shine this attitude pervades into the sexual arena. He need not make his partner feel orgasmic and on a higher place. She will just be grateful he made the effort. In that way that all empaths make excuses she will regard his ineptitude between the sheets as just another item that makes him seem lovable and charming. Okay, he is not the world's best lover, he is not even in the top thousand but he tries and that is all the empath in such a relationship, as this, will want. The empath may just be happy to have someone to share his or her life with and care for. They are not scintillating like me and others that are like me. Accordingly, therefore being a sexual superstar is unnecessary. As I have mentioned in other writings, we are not only creatures of economy but we have been created economically. We do not like to expend energy unnecessarily. It is also the case that if it is not going to gather us fuel we do not need it. In the way that we are not furnished with empathy or the capacity for the remorse, because they do not gather any fuel for us, the low functioning Victim Narcissist is not blessed with sexual prowess, as it serves no purpose for him. He will only seek out those that want to mother him. He will not seek out those who want to be taken to sexual nirvana repeatedly. He will not need to use this sexual weapon to charm his victim because his helplessness and victim status does that for him instead. Accordingly, many of these low functioning narcissists either have little interest in sex or are useless at it.

Sex is still a material factor in the relationship with the Victim Variety because he will exhibit incompetence in this arena so that the caring empath feels sorry for him and will even feel a need to try and teach him. Some narcissists who are of the Victim Variety will go even further and demonstrate varying degrees of frigidity. Once again, this is designed to draw out sympathy from the empath. It is also done to garner sexual attention as well. By exhibiting no interest or little interest in sex or even appearing impotent, the desire to fix will be overwhelming for the empath who will do her best to try to light the fire of desire in this low-functioning narcissist.

The Victim Narcissist will often present with illnesses and ailments. He does not enjoy good health, which is a consequence of him rarely partaking in exercise and his inability to look after himself properly in terms of nutrition and/or hygiene. Not only will he appear with numerous ongoing physical health complaints he will typically invent additional ones in order to draw sympathy and evade having to do things. He has repeated bad backs, injured knees, depression, headache and the like. He is a malingerer and if he cannot point to one of his many ongoing complaints he will readily invent one in order to ensure that the empathic individual that he has ensnared will continue to care for him. You can guarantee that the Victim Narcissist when performing a Hoover (albeit of low intensity and not for a sustained period) will always use the Emergency Power Play and/or the Victim Power Play as part of his portfolio.

You will always find Lesser Victim Narcissists but never any Greater Victim Narcissists. There are occasional Mid-Range Victim Narcissists but the vast majority hail from the lesser school.

The Cerebral Narcissist

The Cerebral Narcissist has a limited interest in sex, certainly of the physical variety. This type of narcissist prefers to flaunt his brilliant intellect as the method by which he seduces his victims. He has little interest in engaging in actual sexual relations because that is not his forte. He has no interest in a remarkable physical appearance because he has no need of it. He need not be toned or slim although it does not always follow that the cerebral narcissist neglects his body to the extent that he becomes some kind of slob. After all, he has suitable awareness and intellect to understand the problems arising from the neglect of his health. He will not be an Adonis but it does not follow that he will be morbidly obese and of questionable hygiene habits. His magnificence stems from his high intellect, his amazing memory and his capacity for complexity. It is the repeated tales of academic achievement, cerebral power and scintillating intellect, which are used to wow and overpower the resistance of his victims. The cerebral narcissist is well read, extensively schooled and excels in showering all who will listen with evidence of his intellectual superiority. Such brilliance proves highly attractive to a certain section of empathic individuals who wish to engage a brain that is the size of a planet. The conversations, albeit one-sided, are nevertheless stimulating and engrossing. There is never a silence for the cerebral narcissist is always primed to provide you with an interesting fact about the champagne that you are both drinking and a historical anecdote concerning the Ponte Vecchio that you are walking over. This walking almanac of facts and opinions is quite dazzling and vastly appealing to some.

The cerebral narcissist will engage in sex periodically if the intellectual avenue becomes exhausted. The sex will not be fulfilling for either party owing to the fact that the cerebral narcissist is neither interested in this nor particularly proficient. It will be done when the intellectual charm is not working as well as it once did and is often done out of a sense of obligation. The cerebral narcissist will feel that every so often he is obligated to discharge his marital responsibilities by engaging in sex with his partner. This is purely done in order to maintain the happiness of the other individual during the golden period and during devaluation, the cerebral narcissist will effectively become frigid, as he will have no interest or sense of obligation to engage in sexual relations with his victim.

The cerebral narcissist however will often talk about sex during the seduction stage. Words are very much the weapons of the narcissist and especially so with the higher functioning of our kin. The cerebral narcissist although uninterested in the physical side of sex, will still wish to show off his vast knowledge of the subject. He will want to regale you with his knowledge of sexual literature, sexual analysis and sexual awareness. He will have read many books about the subject. That is not to enable him to be a better lover but to allow him to be a better speaker about being a lover. The cerebral narcissist will engage in seductive letter writing, often of the old school romantic variety. He will tease and titillate using text messages and telephone messages. He will quite readily, purely for the purpose of seduction, talk dirty down the telephone to you whilst you masturbate. He may tell you he is doing the same but he will not as the physical sensation is of no interest to him. What arouses him is the intellectual power he has in being able to use his lexicon of love to arouse you down the telephone line. Your noises of appreciation and compliments provide him with the fuel he requires, he demonstrates how knowledgeable he is about sex by talking in this manner and he has the added bonus of not having to engage in the actual act. This suits the cerebral narcissist most well. There will be plenty of opportunities for him to exhibit his wide knowledge of sexual practices in order to heighten your anticipation and to wow you as you listen wide-eyed to his explanations of certain techniques and behaviours and what they achieve. He knows all about sex but he certainly does not put it into practice. That is beneath him. In the way that those with a suntan were once looked down upon because this denoted being a manual labourer, the cerebral narcissist looks down on the actual sexual act as beneath him. Why engage in something so crass, something so animalistic and frankly barbaric (other than out of a sense of occasional duty to maintain the façade of the golden period) when one can use the pristine cleanliness of a beautiful mind to gain that all-important fuel? I have a cousin who is a little younger than I am. He is the offspring of my Uncle Peter (who you can read all about in **Fury**) and has been created in the same way as Uncle Peter but he does not have the interest in sex preferring to use his excellent academic credentials and brilliant mind to effect his acquisition of fuel. My cousin finds the act of sexual intercourse so abhorrent because he sees it as beneath someone with such a fine mind as him that on the few occasions he has been compelled to do it, he runs off to the bathroom afterwards and vomits. Not only does he not like the intimacy that comes with the act of coitus but the noise, the fluids, the interaction of parts from which one urinates all disgusts him as he has told me, to my amusement, on many occasions.

The Cerebral Narcissist places significant weight on his intellect being lauded and recognised. He excels in sitting and passing exams and will have a string of qualifications in order to brow beat any opponent before the debate has begun. He is more qualified ergo he is superior. The Cerebral Narcissist places considerable value on his intellectual achievements being recognised and any failure to do so will ignite his fury. He cannot stand ignorance. He will correct people when they speak, revel in revealing they are incorrect about a fact and lobe nothing more than to hold forth and argue with people. For him more than any other cadre narcissist words are the essence of his being. He loves the economy that accompanies their use, he delights in the effect they have both in seduction and devaluation and his superiority must always be recognised.

The Cerebral Narcissist, in the same way that he is disinterested in his body and the sexual arena, has no interest in physical abuse. It will take a severe loss of control, possibly on entering the Chaos Mode or alternatively following sustained criticisms whereby the fury is ignited, for a Cerebral Narcissist to use physical abuse against his or her victim. It will tend to be grabbing, pushing and holding down as opposed to punching and kicking. The Cerebral Narcissist is also aware of the evidential ramifications arising from physical abuse and is too clever (unless control has been lost) to engage in such behaviours. He regards physical abuse as beneath him, preferring to engage in the fine art of emotional and psychological abuse.

The Cerebral Narcissist is an extensive user of Lieutenants. His innate charisma combined with his intellect enables him to recruit and manipulate others. Since he shuns the body, he prefers others to do the donkeywork and is entirely content to recruit them to do this on his behalf. He will carry out much of his work by proxy, seeing it as beneath him to become involved in the minutiae of the abuse but rather he is there to plan it, orchestrate it and command it.

Naturally you will not find any Lesser Cerebral Narcissists. They are drawn both from the ranks of the Mid-Range school whereby the Cerebral Narcissist will exhibit all the traits explained above but will lack any malign intent. Those Greater Cerebral Narcissists are dangerous individuals. Their higher function combined with their emphasis on the mind mean that all manner of manipulative tools will be used against you during seduction and devaluation. The Greater Cerebral Narcissist is Machiavellian in approach, covert and extremely manipulative. All narcissists lie but he is the Chief of Lies. Words are his speciality and it follows that in unleashing his malevolent campaign against you lies will be used extensively. In fact, it is fair to say that he will issue more lies than truth and thus makes for a most dangerous opponent.

The Somatic Narcissist

Here comes the gym bunny that has a bottom so tight it will bounce off the walls before he bounces you all around the bedroom. The Somatic Narcissist is obsessed with his or her physical appearance. They diet fastidiously, put the hours in at the gym, select the clothing which allows them to flaunt their bodies and spend a lot of time with their favourite person; their reflection in the mirror. They look for reactions of admiration to their beauty, their physical perfection, their muscular appearance and smart and attractive appearances. The Somatic Narcissist likes to demonstrate athletic ability by showing his body can throw the furthest, run the fastest or dive the deepest. The appearance of his or her body and what can be achieved through it (strength, flexibility, and endurance) are what matter in order to draw fuel from their victims.

This fixation with the body means that the arena of sex is hugely important to the Somatic Narcissist. He wants to look terrific whilst having sex so you coo and purr over that finely honed body, the impressive biceps and rigid six-pack. Not only that but look at how he can have sex for a long time as he flips you from this position to the next like a piece of meat. His stamina is legendary, his ability to get you and him into all manner of positions should be respected and admired and all of this is achieved whilst looking like a Greek god. Whereas the cerebral narcissist uses his intellect to conquer, the somatic narcissist uses his or her body to achieve the same outcome. His body is designed for admiration and where better to achieve that than in the bedroom.

The Somatic Narcissist will also demonstrate the legendary hypocrisy for which we are known. You must not compete with him in any way in the looks department but you are expected to look your best because you are an extension of him. You must not gain weight, have bad skin, wear ill-fitting clothes or forget to shave your legs. You must walk the tightrope of ensuring that you fit in with his image of bodily perfection whilst at the same time not pulling the spotlight away from him. The Somatic Narcissist will excel during the seductive stage because the twin allure of somebody looking so good and performing so brilliantly between the sheets will blow you away. You will receive premium quality sex, amazing orgasms, grade A sexual encounters. His stamina is vast, his eagerness and readiness to copulate is staggering and you will be the beneficiary in all of this. This is just a fortunate coincidence for you because as with all types of our kind, the Somatic Narcissist is just after your fuel. You may not regard this as such a problem during the seduction phase. So what if he gets off on your screams of pleasure and your repeated appreciation of those defined forearms and pectoral muscles, you are being given the sexual time of your life, he deserves the praise doesn't he? Naturally, this is how we want it to work. You give us the fuel, have no realisation what you are doing, and therefore have no concern, so consequently you embrace it wholeheartedly. When the devaluation occurs, you can expect the somatic narcissist to maintain still a rampant sexual appetite but the last thing on his mind will be making you purr with pleasure. You will be taken against your will, subjected to lengthy sexual hammerings as he focuses on how brilliant he is at lasting so long, how glorious his taut muscles look as he ploughs away at you. There is no consideration for whether you are enjoying yourself or even if you are being physically hurt because all that matters to him is how good he looks and how masterful he is in the sack. If you were to vanish from beneath him, he would barely notice. The somatic narcissist is in effect having sex with himself. He is so fine to look at that he would eat himself if he could and similarly he would engage in sexual intercourse with himself if that were a possibility. Masturbation ranks high with narcissists anyway but this action is even more prevalent with the somatic narcissist. He will position himself in front a mirror and as he plays with himself, he will admire how he looks and this reinforces his need for you to admire him also. The somatic narcissist will bombard you with pictures of his buff body and his penis during the seduction stage. He will also do this with online strangers in order to gain their admiration also.

Exhibiting their physicality is necessary for the somatic variety of our kind. Accordingly, you can expect sexual gymnastics during the seduction phase and then to be slapped, smacked, bent over, throttled, pinned down and all other manifestations of physical dominance. The fear in your eyes as he pins you to the bed and takes what he regards as his only goes to fuel him further. Any kind of treatment, which emphasises his physical prowess and superiority, will be meted out in the sexual arena and invariably you will suffer consequently. You can expect to be humiliated, dominated and shoved around by the somatic narcissist during devaluation. You are little more than a blow-up doll to him, which is to be manipulated into all manner of positions all in order to make him look magnificent. You are expected to be grateful for the sexual pounding you have received and if your praise is not forthcoming then expect the consequences, as this inherent criticism will ignite his rage. Rather than rely on withering put downs and caustic comments, the somatic narcissist will lash out physically, again underpinning his physical superiority whilst storing away your transgression for use in the sexual arena at a later date. The somatic narcissist will insist on bondage, your subjugation being a natural consequence of his superiority. You will be bent over his knee and smacked with his hand or a cane. I know of one narcissist who would apply nettles to his scrotum because he explained it gave him a massive and sustained erection, notwithstanding the pain and he expected his victim to endure the application of those nettles to her nipples, bottom and thighs in order to heighten her sexual experience also. In the hands of the somatic narcissist, sex is a highly charged weapon. It is with the somatic narcissist that you will experience the greatest highs during the sexual seduction and the humiliating and hurtful lows when the devaluation occurs.

The Somatic Narcissist lets his or body do the talking and therefore words whilst used by the Somatic Narcissist are used less extensively and with less impact than if they were being wielded by the Cerebral Narcissist. You will find that much of what the Somatic Narcissist will say will revolve around how magnificent he or she looks, material items, his or new car, the new house they have bought or the new extension to a house. The material and the tangible are what matter to the Somatic Narcissist and accordingly money, expensive items and events are high on their list of priorities. It is all about how it looks. They like to appear magnificent both in their appearance and the environment in which they operate. They are the epitome of showing off the shiny and the sparkling as part of their approach to seduce and beguile you. During devaluation you can expect all of the beautiful things to be withdrawn and for their words to focus on how you have lost your looks, gained weight, how you are not caring about your appearance anymore, that you are failing to keep the house tidy and such like. Much of what the Somatic Narcissist will say will revolve around appearance and presentation.

There are no Lesser Somatic Narcissists. Their lack of interest in their environment, lower functioning and general poor physical appearance and health do not equate to the Somatic Narcissist. The Mid Range Somatic Narcissist is still rampant in their sexual appetite, their desire for all to look beautiful and their obsession with looks. They will however lack the drive and malignant nature of the Greater Somatic Narcissist. This creature is a lady-killer or a seductive siren. Utterly vain, compellingly beautiful or handsome he or she knows that to look upon them is to look upon the beauty of heaven. They regard their beauty as captivating. They turn heads, stop traffic and have people fall in love with them from the moment they set eyes on him or her. The Greater Somatic Narcissist has an incredible sexual appetite from the get go and uses this to stun their victim into submission. By equal turns they will wrench it away from their victim once the malign nature is unleashed. The Greater Somatic Narcissist is a cruel creature, entranced by their own image and someone who is all too ready to lambaste others who fall beneath their ridiculously high standards. The Greater Somatic Narcissist is an occasion when beauty has never been so ugly.

The Elite Narcissist

The final category of narcissist is the Elite Narcissist. He combines both the looks and physical supremacy of the Somatic Narcissist with the intellect and spoken charm of the Cerebral Narcissist. The Elite Narcissist will talk you into bed and deliver as well. He will have your mind aroused and then your body. He may not be quite the sexual champion that the Somatic Narcissist is but he is no slouch. He will look after himself and be trim and athletic if not ripped and buff, but such a look is not beyond him. He may not have the total cranial magnificence of the Cerebral Narcissist but again he is no dribbling idiot. He has plenty of intelligence and wit, which he puts to good use. This combination of intelligence and looks creates the deadliest narcissist because he can use to both charm and seduce you and then use both to devalue you. Hence, he is categorised as an elite member of our club.

The Elite Narcissist is interested in sex because he recognises that sex comes in many forms. He knows that is can be the sensual whisper in your ear or the raunchy text messaging he sends you. He knows it is the athletic and sudden performance in a penthouse suit and the gentle, tender lovemaking that you crave. He has none of the disgust for the sexual act like the Cerebral Narcissist and does not rely solely on physical domination like the Somatic Narcissist. He is able to combine both worlds and straddle the same in order to exact his manipulations. Where the mouth leads, his body will follow and you are subjected to the one-two combination. Whilst the Victim Narcissist needs the mothering empath, the Cerebral Narcissist needs the disciple empath who worships at this temple of knowledge, the Somatic Narcissist needs the empath who is swayed by looks, and the Elite

Narcissist just needs somebody with empathic qualities. They may not be a complete empath but the everyday charm and attractiveness of the Elite Narcissist will seduce someone who may have lower empathic qualities than normal and this in turn provides the Elite Narcissist with access to a larger pool of potential victims. Naturally, the Elite Narcissist will be using sex (in word and deed) to ensnare an empath, a super-empath or a co-dependent but he is able to mine fuel from some of the lesser prospects. The Elite Narcissist will use the spoken charm and knowledge of the Cerebral Narcissist and meld it with the sexual physical allure of the Somatic Narcissist to create a very potent sexual magnet indeed. Few can resist him and the sex he grants is gratifying on many levels. For the same reason, when the Elite Narcissist commences the devaluation, his victim his subjected to a further double whammy as spoken word and physical act are used against her. The effect is devastating.

The Elite Narcissist stalks the world with his double-barrel of capabilities to charm and ensnare and when the time is right he can turn that double-barrel on his victim and unleash not one but two forms of devastating devaluation. This cadre of narcissist is very difficult to resist. Although it may look like an oxymoron there are Mid-Range Elite Narcissists. This means that those who combine looks and intellect do so with particular effect but they do so without the drive and malign intent of those from the Greater school. They perform effective Hoovers, which are sustained and intense because the Elite Narcissist has combined two cadres of narcissist, which gives him or her more tools to apply, more manipulations to administer and a greater prospect of ensnaring their victim once again. Those that are without the malign influence will move on to a different victim should the current target exhibit a slavish devotion to No Contact.

Ultimately there is the Greater Elite Narcissist. This malevolent and malign creature will seduce you with a double whammy of looks and intellect, whisk you off your feet in seconds and be the toast of everyone you know. You will be regarded as having secured the golden ticket to the golden period and in utter nirvana. As ever the higher you climb the greater your fall and when the Greater Elite Narcissist unleashes his or campaign of vitriolic devaluation against you, you will need to get far away if you are ever to escape him or her. The Grand Hoover deployed by the Greater Elite Narcissist is of hurricane force as every conceivable method of manipulation is hurled at you in a fearsome bid to cause you to capitulate. Even if, somehow, you manage to survive the Grand Hoover you will be subjected to repeated attempts to draw you back in. No matter what other fuel the Greater Elite Narcissist has acquired he or she will still dedicate time and energy to your downfall. They will not rest until one day they have secured that potent Hoover fuel from you. It may be tomorrow of in fifteen years but they will always come after you.

Accordingly, having an understanding of which cadre of narcissist you are dealing with and from what school they are drawn is highly relevant. Not only does this allow you to understand the nature of your relationship with them it allows you insight into the crucial steps of devaluation and Hoover. Going beyond this, for the purposes of achieving your revenge it also allows you to comprehend just how much work you have ahead of you. I mentioned in the chapter above that there are eight narcissistic pillars, which form your targets. It is these pillars that you must topple in order to secure your revenge. Not all of these pillars are applicable to the cadres and schools of narcissist, some contain all of the pillars and others fewer. In order to assist you in knowing how many pillars you will have to topple I shall list each category of narcissist and the number of pillars that are applicable to that category.

Category	Number
Lesser Victim Narcissist	Five pillars
Mid-Range Victim Narcissist	Six pillars
Mid-Range Cerebral Narcissist	Six pillars
Greater Cerebral Narcissist	Eight pillars
Mid-range Somatic Narcissist	Seven pillars
Greater Somatic Narcissist	Eight pillars
Mid-range Elite Narcissist	Seven pillars
Greater Elite Narcissist	Eight pillars

I am not going to tell you at this juncture which ones are missing in the instances where there are less than eight pillars as I will let you work that out as you read through each description of the pillars. I will then confirm to you which pillars are applicable to which category of narcissist. You have to do some work here too you know. You will see that even the black sheep of the narcissistic brethren, the Lesser Victim Narcissist has five pillars so in achieving a proper revenge over the narcissist there is much to do in terms of what to target.

Thus you know understand the type of narcissist you are dealing with, the qualities they exhibit, the danger they pose to you and how many of the narcissistic pillars you will need to topple in order to secure your ultimate aim and achieve revenge over the narcissist in your life. It is time to turn our attention to explain what each of the eight pillars is before we move onto the crucial part of explaining to you how you go about toppling each of these eight pillars. You may know some or all of them. You may know them by slightly different names or labels but either way you will be able to recognise them and understand why they are so fundamental to us. In some instances, they will bleed into one another, sharing some elements but they remain distinct and form to us the very backbone of our existence, the core of our being here and the touchstone for our being. We now turn to the Eight Narcissistic Pillars. Now the targets for your revenge come into sight.

6 The Narcissistic Pillars

We will examine each of the eight narcissistic pillars, as you must understand what they are and what each involves if you are to then be able to topple them and achieve the ultimate aim as part of your revenge. It is worth pointing out that the pillars are linked to one another. They support one another and are connected. I will identify these connections as I work through them and no doubt you will be able to establish where one works with another to create and underpin what we believe ourselves to be. This is an important point to be aware of since once you begin to target these narcissistic pillars and damage them, not only will you affect the pillar you have targeted you will be causing collateral damage to the adjoining and connecting pillars. In the same way we go after fuel irrespective of the cost and consequence to those around us, causing additional damage as our tornado of destruction surges through people's lives you will also be generating such side effects in your attacks on the narcissistic pillars. This is turn will provide you with considerable satisfaction and is a key part of the campaign to secure your revenge over the narcissist.

6.1 The First Pillar - Status

Our status and standing in the world is of considerable importance to us. This will manifest in us requiring suitably grand sounding job titles to herald our importance to the business that we are involved in. In the United Kingdom we will hanker have recognition in the honour lists by seeking the addition of letters after our names, being knighted or elevated to the position of a lord. For us status is conveyed through the size of our house and its location, the number of bathrooms it has and the extent and quality of the furnishings through out it. There is no better example than demonstrating our kind's fixation with the quality of items ranging from watches to which dry cleaner to use than in Bret Easton Ellis' American Psycho. Patrick Bateman is most certainly a Greater Elite Narcissist. Our clothes must reflect our standing. Our haircuts, manicures, attendances at tanning salon, the whiteness of our teeth, the scope and extent of our library collection of books, the ornaments displayed through our home, our music and blu-ray collection and so on and so forth. We must be a member of elite and lofty clubs ranging from the best country club to the most prestigious gold club. We hold an executive box at the football stadium. We always sit in the corporate entertainment facility at concerts. We must have the best seats in a restaurant. Our cruise cabin has to always be seaward. Our hotel room in a coastal resort must have a sea view. Our car must be impressive; indeed, there should be cars. Public transport is beneath us other than the use of taxis and then only rarely since a limousine should be used to effect a suitable entrance. From the shoes on our feet to the product used on our hair everything will reek of quality and status. We may invariably be crass about it and that is why so many of our kind emerge from the recently moneyed, the grasping middle classes and the nouveau riche. Those who have status but are not obsessed by it rarely mention it. They dress in mustard corduroys and scarlet jumpers, which have a hole in the arm. The collars of their shirts are frayed but none of these matters to them because they have no need to herald who and what they are to the world. We do. Our status is fundamental to our sense of who we are. We expect preferential treatment. We do not expect to queue anywhere. We fraternise with the rich and famous as we frantically pull strips from them to adorn our own construct, which is wrapped around this first pillar of status.

Status is very important to us and we must ensure that others are aware of our status. Our letterheads will refer to any letters we may have after our name or any elevated title we have. We will remove the number from our address and call the property by a name such as 'The Rectory' or 'The Fold' or 'The Old Lodge'. Nothing as crass as 'Dunroamin' of course. We will look to employ a staff wherever possible from gardener through to nanny and cook. Our home must look like a show home ready for a television crew to walk through it. Our social calendar requires attendance at marquee events in the local community and beyond. We must attend the well-regarded balls, which take place, the dinner dances and fetes. We see the value in charitable work also in order to not only maintain our façade but to ensure that others see how kind and caring we are. Not only this but such works are likely to put us in line for awards and titles based on our selfless charity work. Of course you will never find us working in the soup kitchen or rattling a tin in a supermarket on a cold Saturday morning. No, that is beneath our status but we will provide the ideas and orchestrate the campaigns in order for the little people to then go out and effect them.

The Cerebral of our kind will want a long list of academic publications to their name and a securely tenured position at a prestigious university or research institution. The Somatic will point to sporting achievements, cups and trophies proudly displayed to demonstrate their sporting prowess. We will aim to own extensive collections of rare vinyl records, jewellery, weapons and so on, all of which will be displayed to allow the visitor to our collection to understand the significance of this collection and how in turn it increases our status.

At work I will have the largest team working for me, the office with best view and most expensive office furniture. I will have a group of minions running around for me. Access to the executive washroom, a coveted car-parking space in the basement car park and other such perks which denote my elevated status.

Status through material possessions and accomplishments are absolutely crucial to us. We place great value in this being a cornerstone of our existence and letting the world know that this is the case. This narcissistic pillar of status will be a target for you to topple in your revenge campaign.

6.2 Entitlement

Our sense of entitlement is huge and thus it forms the second narcissistic pillar. Naturally somebody who holds an elevated position in this world, who is special and of a high status is entitled to many things. Even without such status we regard ourselves as different and special and therefore entitled to be treated in a preferential fashion, looked after and afforded what ever we want, when we want and where ever we want it. This sense of entitlement is behind our well know lack of regard for other people's boundaries. We always park our tanks on other people's lawns. This sense of entitlement allows us to act as we please. It is what is behind our absence of consideration for others, the removal of guilt and the omission of remorse. Why would we ever feel sorrow and guilt for something we have done when we are perfectly entitled to have behaved that way? Moreover, this sense of entitlement is necessary for the preservation of our existence. We are entitled to fuel because we need it. We are entitled to get it from whom we want in whatever method we choose. It does not matter whether we con or hurt this person, smother them in false flattery or strike them down with vile words and actions, it must be done because we are entitled to act this way.

Entitlement bleeds into the concept of status as well. We are entitled to belong to certain clubs, organisations and bodies because they are for people like us. We want to belong to these establishments in order to fraternise with the great and the good and in turn avail ourselves of the opportunity to tear from them certain shards and segments to apply to our own construct. By belonging to such organisations we are reinforcing our special status and we entirely believe that we are entitled to belong. Whether it is the golf club or an exclusive gym we must belong and we will ensure that achieving that membership fulfills our sense of entitlement. We will usually charm our way into achieving inclusion but we are not above deploying darker methods to ensure that our sense of entitlement is met. We will threaten, intimidate and blackmail to ensure we get what we want. We have spent our lives with this sense of entitlement and nobody is going to get in our way as we continue to pursue it.

This sense of entitlement pervades everything that we do. We can say what we want to people because we know we are entitled to the fuel that flows from their reaction (either good or bad) and that because we are special we are in a position to pass comment on anyone and everything. This entitlement manifests in us having an opinion on everything. We are entitled to pass judgement on your new outfit, a person's choice of car, what they have selected from the menu, their political views, their preferred book and so forth. We are self-proclaimed experts in every field and will spout our views whether people wish to hear them or not. If we have a rapt and attentive audience we gain positive fuel from these people and their admiring noises and glances, the applause and the earnest questions as they seek to tap into our knowledge. Should those assembled prove hostile we are just as content, so long as our façade is not damaged, for their negative reaction provides us with fuel. Thus we feel we are entitled to be provocative with certain groups of people, especially those who are not part of our façade. We will go out of our way to rile others when we are not reliant on them to accept the façade. Insulting and putting down others not only demonstrates again our lack of respect for people's boundaries but forms part of our entitlement.

Our entitlement means we start from the top. We cannot be expected to work from the bottom and make our way upward. We are entitled to a higher position than normal within an organisation. We expect people to do what we want irrespective of how ridiculous our demand might be. This will often manifest in our dealings with minions where we demand extra special treatment in our hotel or at a restaurant. Our dry cleaning must go to the front of the queue, our purchases should always come gift-wrapped and we should never need a reservation at a restaurant, as they should be delighted to accommodate us whenever we arrive. This entitlement means that rules do not apply to us. From the minor rules such as not talking loudly in a library or using a mobile phone in the quiet carriage on the train all the way through conventions, procedures, regulations up to the laws of the land. We can file our tax return when we see fit as we are entitled to do so and if he authorities try to give us a hard time well we will seek special treatment and blame someone else for the lateness that has arisen.

We expect people to be far more interested in us than we are in them. Again our desires, achievements and interests are always far more interesting than anything you say or do. This is because we are entitled to act in this way because we are elevated and special. We can behave as we wish by not honouring appointments, failing to give notice when we cancel an arrangement and insisting that others organise their arrangements around us. If a store is about to close, we will demand to be served. We may know that a service provider needs to leave to get to the next appointment but we will not let them until we are satisfied that our entitlement has been fulfilled by making them stay and attend to our petty inconveniences.

Our sense of entitlement is behind our capacity to freeload. Whilst we may exhibit generosity and largesse when it suits us in order to create a favourable impression in order to seduce and/or maintain the façade, wherever possible we will take advantage of others so that we do not have to use our own resources. We will depart suddenly before the end of an evening to avoid paying our share of the drinks bill or if we know someone will pay for dinner for us we will choose the most expensive items and order too much for us to eat. We will look to obtain free entry to attractions, obtain free advice from people even though that is how they make their living. We will take more than our allotted time at events in order to squeeze out more for ourselves irrespective of how that may affect other people. We will borrow items and never return them and then pretend that the items belonged to us all along. Should we damage property belonging to another we will never replace the broken item. We will not pay back money since we believe we are entitled to keep it, after all you get our friendship don't you and that is worth more than the several thousand pounds that you have leant to us.

Our sense of entitlement means we get to know everything about you. You are afforded no privacy. We expect to know your passwords so we can see what is on your phone, we will open your post, read your e-mails and invade any element of privacy. We will listen in on your conversations; interrupt discussions you are having with other people. We will turn up when we have not been invited to keep an eye on you and find out what is going on. We will always be questioning what you are doing, who with and why. You are not able to keep anything away from us because we are entitled to know.

This sense of entitlement drives much of our unpleasant behaviour. From our entitlement to fuel through to our entitlement to control you and invade your life. It is vulgar, intrusive and never-ending and as a consequence a huge sense of entitlement forms the second of the narcissistic pillars.

6.3 Omnipotence

Omnipotence is the quality of possessing unlimited or very great power and we know that this is entirely applicable to us. We regard ourselves as a god that strides the earth demonstrating this vast power that we have. The little people look upon us with awe and admiration and later fear and terror at the unrivalled and massive power that we wield.

Our kind, especially the greater variety, regards what we do as a film with us as the star. All the cameras are trained on us as a stirring and dramatic soundtrack accompanies our every move. This sense of drama is only fitting for one so powerful as me. I am impregnable, my powers of seduction are irresistible and my ability to destroy is magnificent in its effectiveness. You cannot help but be impressed by the power that I hold. I can bend people's wills so that they carry out my bidding. I possess a super natural capacity to sniff out and sense those that will serve me with greatest loyalty and provide me the best and most succulent fuel. My senses are a hundred fold increased beyond yours. My black eyes will seek out and identify a victim within moments of entering an environment. I can taste the fuel that drips from them as I near them, savouring that sweet tang as I contemplate driving my hooks deep into them and commencing the extraction of the fuel. I listen to every word that passes your lips. Like some kind of sorting machine, my ears draw in the sounds you make allowing me to extract fuel from your noises of admiration and praise, your compliments and your words of love and affection. I also pluck that which you tell me in your incessant rambling, which will serve a purpose for me. Like someone panning for gold I locate with ease those nuggets of intelligence, which tell me about the things you enjoy, the things you desire and the things, which frighten you. I sift through your invective, extracting your weaknesses and vulnerabilities and storing them in my vast mind, logging the information, which will be called on in a flash to use against you. My touch reassures, lures and caresses as my extensive tendrils wrap around you. Seductive words spill from my mouth as I say everything you want to hear, my choice of sentence causing you such delight and stirring up those emotions of love, desire and affection. You are in the presence of a god and your fragile form is being dashed upon the rocks of my brilliance. You will break against me, any resistance that you might have being extinguished as this weapon of mass seduction triumphs. I am a one-man army, which invades your world and conquers it. In time you will bear testament to my many triumphs, a history of subjugation and assimilation as I smash through barriers and claim that which is mine by right. Nobody can stand in my way. Nobody is able to resist me. I come with the clamour of sound, the brightness of light and the frenetic energy, which lifts you off your feet and draws you deep into my vortex yet you have no idea what I am. That is how powerful I am. Defenders of a country know to look out for invading soldiers, marauding paratroopers, armoured vehicles and aircraft. I unleash my love missiles in your direction, order the carpet love bombing of your person, deploy my tanks to bludgeon their way into your life and a hundred other weapons of seduction and you never see them coming. Your defences are useless when faced with my might. You are defenceless. Even if you could muster some form of resistance it would be overcome so readily by one as mighty as I.

Yet my power does not end there. I have the ability to make everyone admire me, not just you. I will charm your friends, your family, your colleagues and all who come into contact with me. I spread my magic amongst them and watch as they each come under my spell one by one. I have them carry out my works for me, charming you further, heralding my might. Like trumpeters they announce my arrival with great ceremony, which is befitting one so mighty as I. This power flows through me; it crackles around me and sparks from me. Like some thunderous giant I am able, with most malevolent fury, unleash this power to crush my foes. Those who seek to oppose me, if they cannot be charmed, then they will be smitten and returned into the dust from which they came. I will hammer you into near oblivion as I continue to extract fuel from you. I am king of a hundred manipulations such is my power. I will have you blinded, deafened and number as I control your sense. I will make you dance for me, jig for me and do anything that I want. I will possess you with this unrivalled power that only I possess. Recognise this power to seduce and to abuse. See how when I have left you broken and reduced to near nothingness I am able, though my vast power to resurrect you once again and draw you back to me. Who else possesses such a power to shatter and individual and then put them back together again. Am I not a god for exhibiting such ability? Kneel before me and worship my greatness and pay homage to my omnipotence. Let others know of my brilliance and sacrifice your everything on the altar that has been built in tribute to me.

These powers that I wield, over you and so many others, can only belong to a god. Of that there can be no doubt. I have been placed on this earth to test you and I will always find you wanting for you cannot even hope to equate to a fraction of what I am. This is power. Raw, visceral and complete. The knowledge of what I am enables me to gather my fuel and achieve my aims.

This sense of omnipotence that I describe is a crucial element and drives much of the behaviours that we exhibit. This sense of power is fundamental to our existence. It sets us apart from all others and allows us to do what is necessary to maintain our supply of fuel. By attacking our sense of omnipotence and rendering impotent you will be striking a massive blow against us when you topple this third narcissistic pillar. I have little doubt after reading all about this power your desire for revenge has been heightened, as you want to see that pillar topple and for me to fall.

6.4 Superiority

We are superior to all of those around us and most of all we are superior to you. This innate sense of superiority is crucial to our existence. Not only do we believe this to be entirely correct but also it is a state we must always maintain. Our belief in our superiority is reinforced by the existence of the other pillars. If we were not so superior how is it, then we are able to do as we please and when we please (entitlement)? If our superiority did not exist how then is it that we are able to achieve so much and be held in high regard (status)? The fact that we exhibit such power (omnipotence) is testament to the fact that we are superior. We are dedicated to this concept because like the other narcissistic pillars it provides the engine by which we can achieve our goal of securing fuel.

As a superior being we have been created differently from you. You are burdened with guilt, worry, remorse and having to care for others. Do not get me wrong, my kind and me are delighted that you are since this means you will provide us with fuel and you will be hindered in your attempts to escape us. We however have not been built to suffer the sting of shame, the debilitating effects of worry or the weight of remorse. We are not concerned with having to care for others. The reason for this is because all of these things and other attributes besides will act as diversions and distractions from our goals of acquiring fuel. The very fact that we have been created with these weaknesses underlines once again our superiority.

Our heightened ability to charm and seduce is yet more evidence of our superiority. The fact that we are able to abuse someone and yet they still do not leave us, instead they cling on and clamour for a return to the golden period. Only a superior individual can achieve this. We are achievers in our chosen fields. Captains of industry, charismatic politicians, entertaining chat show hosts, dazzling pop stars, capable and effective professionals at the top of our game, outstanding authors, scintillating artists, magnificent sportsmen and women. This is all evidence that we are superior.

Even those of our kind who do not hit the heady heights of intellectual, physical or career achievement know they are at least superior to you. That central tenet is something we know to be the case but moreover it is also something we will ensure remains the case. The maintenance of our superiority is a fundamental driver for the devaluation that we subject you to. When you admire and love us you are recognising our natural superiority in a variety of ways. For some reason, over time, you neglect to pay homage to this superiority as often as you ought and with the intensity you once did. This means that not only do we suffer a reduction in our fuel but we also feel a loss of our superiority. By devaluing you we reinstate the provision of quality fuel from provoking and evoking negative emotional reactions from you but we are also able to reassert our superiority.

Our manipulative tools are designed to ensure that you realise that we are the one who is in control and therefore that we are superior to you. We are the ones which call the shots, make the decisions and govern your lives and you had best remember this otherwise you will suffer the consequences. So much of your daily interaction with ourselves is designed to enable us to assert and maintain our superiority. Consider the following: -

- You are expected to undertaken menial chores and we do not help
- The times we talk over you
- The times we correct what you are saying
- The occasions we upbraid you in front of other people for not doing something correctly or saying the wrong thing
- How we have you running around after us but not the other way around

- All major decisions concerning finance, household etc must be taken by us and not you. Your opinion is not worth having.
- The repeated occasions we show off about our achievements, knowledge and accomplishments
- We never praise or even acknowledge what you achieve
- We never comment on what you contribute to the relationship and the household despite you doing the lion's share of the work

All of these points and others are factors in keeping you believing that you are inferior to us. Our sense of superiority is predicated on two factors and these are important for you to keep in mind when we address toppling this particular pillar in the chapter below. The first factor is we look to our inflated ego and our exaggerated achievements as evidence of our superiority. The second factor is by reinforcing your inferiority we become superior by default even if we did not have those achievements and accomplishments, which we brag about so often. Imagine that a wall represents our superiority based on achievement, who we portray ourselves to be and so on. That wall looks high. Now did a moat beneath it, representing your inferiority and stand in the bottom of the moat. The wall now appears twice as high. By undermining you, putting you down and repeatedly denigrating you we are able to exaggerate our own sense of superiority.

Thus the fourth narcissistic pillar hinges on our sense of superiority both innate and compared to the inferior nature of who you are.

6.5 Lack of Accountability

It is a well-known fact that our kind does not do accountability. Once again the presence of the other pillars will make itself known in this regard. Why would we ever be accountable when we are so powerful (omnipotence), better than you and everyone else (superiority) able to do as we please without hindrance or restraint (entitlement) and beyond reproach owing to our special nature (status). Once again the inter-connection of the pillars is evidenced. They are linked to one another and support and reinforce each other, but by virtue of that connection they also have the capacity to weaken one another.

We are not accountable to our actions. We do not answer to others for what we do because we are beyond this. You are inferior and that is why you are called to account in so many ways. You are responsible for the outcomes resulting from your decisions and actions at work. You are accountable for how you bring your children up. You must explain yourself when questioned by an authority figure. Not only does this happen because you are an inferior person it is also integral to who you are as an empathic individual. Since you are burdened by guilt and caring you are an apologist and feel the need to explain your actions to people. You must understand a situation, comprehend why a person has behaved in a certain way and by the same token you prefer to explain yourself and ensure that people understand why you have acted the way you have. This need and desire to explain causes you to become accountable. This does not apply to us. We never feel any need to explain why we have said what we have said or to have people understand why we have behaved in a certain way. We are above having to do this. Such behaviour is for the likes of you. Having to explain oneself is a hindrance and we must be free of hindrances in order to gather our fuel. We are blessed by the fact that we are always right and therefore there is never any need for our decisions to be questioned. We do not appreciate being held to account as to do so is to suggest that we are less than that which we think we are. It is to suggest we are like you and we know that is not the case.

This lack of accountability and responsibility manifests in many different ways. This includes the following: -

- Behaving as we want
- Ignoring rules and conventions
- Never accepting blame
- Never apologising
- Not helping in any scenario be it work or home
- Having no regard for legal process
- Making and then breaking agreements
- Failing to pay in respect of obligations such as bills, child support and spousal maintenance
- Repeatedly lying to maintain the avoidance of accountability
- Challenging those in authority

If consequences arise from our actions,
 which others try and hold us to account for them we will reject those assertions. The key component to maintaining this lack of accountability is denial. We will deny something has happened so it cannot be attributed to us. We will deny we had anything to do with it, we were not there, and we did cause the thing to happen or that it was not our fault. We deny and deny again.

Denial is a necessary mechanism. It is necessary for healthy people as a defence mechanism. It is necessary for me as a manipulative technique. For you, an obvious example would be the death of a loved one. You are overwhelmed by this loss. In order to protect your mind in the light of this emotional shock, you may go into a state of denial, namely you deny that your spouse or mother has died. This enables you to cope with the shock of the event until your mind is able to then deal with the loss.

Do not make the mistake of thinking that when I deny something it is because deep down I am in pain as a consequence of my behaviour and similar to the example above, I am denying the behaviour to try and deal with the pain. This is incorrect. I am not in pain as a result of what I have done. I do not regard whatever act it is I have committed, as something that is bad, hence there is no pain. I deny to manipulate you and I deny to avoid accountability.

- Denial allows me to avoid accountability because you will give up your attack against me
- I make you feel bad for attacking me as a consequence of this denial
- I continue to do what I want and thus my freedom from accountability continues.

I will lie and deny that I have done anything wrong. I will keep on denying it. I will repeatedly deny what you are accusing me of and I will keep going. I should have been a politician such is my ability to deny what is right in front of me. My shutters down and stonewall defence is impregnable. It becomes wearing for you to keep repeating your accusation against me. In the end you will become fed up and just stop. Accordingly, I have defeated your attack against me without any admission of wrongdoing or accountability on my part.

The insistence of my denials then has the effect of making you feel like you have done something wrong. You have failed to show that I have been guilty of what you have accused me of. You are accordingly prejudicial, unfair, judgemental and hectoring. Moreover, your failure to achieve an outcome, by which you wish to hold me to account, which would ordinarily result in an admission by me, means that I have not accepted what I did, was wrong. Nor have you been able to prove what I did was wrong. I regard that as validation that what I had done was permissible and acceptable, clearing the way for me to go and do it again. This perpetuates my lack of accountability.

I deploy differing techniques of denial. I will usually flatly deny that what has happened actually did happen. This is where I like to unveil my very good friend, plausible deniability. I can sense when you have some doubt and I will drive a truck filled with uncertainty through that chink of doubt in order to blow apart your accusations. Alternatively, I will question your recall of the event. Again, when I scent a degree of confusion on your part I will seize on it and hammer home the message that you have got it wrong. This becomes more and more useful since the more you start to doubt yourself, the more often I will exploit this and I will also remind you of your previous memory failings in a bid to convince you that once again you are incorrect.

Try and refer to someone else to support your castigation of me and I will avoid that too. If somehow you have avoided speaking to one of my Lieutenants and instead you have enlisted the support of someone untouched by my corrupting charm, I will deny they are entitled to sit in judgement of me.

"Oh Louise says I did it did she? Well she would. You know she is jealous that you and me are together. Did you not know that? (Why not throw in some Triangulation too) Yes, she has been after me for ages. I am surprised you haven't noticed. She is just doing this to try and split us up. Do you want her to do that?"

Thus, I deny that Louse has any valid basis for supporting your criticism and she is denied as evidence in your case against me.

A different way for me to deny the validity of what you are saying is to compare my behaviour to something worse. You criticise me for forgetting an anniversary when you have remembered it. I cannot deny that this has happened so I will again attack the validation of your standpoint in a similar fashion to the above. However, on this occasion I will seek to remove your validity by trivialising your complaint.

"Oh have you heard yourself? It is just an anniversary. It wasn't even an important one. It was only three years. Good grief, it's not as if someone has died is it? You are carrying on as if there has been a mass murder of your family. You need to get some perspective."

I will follow this up with some choice observations such as

"You are too sensitive"
"You are always on my case"
"It wasn't that bad"
"You are making a mountain out of a molehill. Again."

One of my favourite retorts when you are seeking to blame me or you are trying to get me to admit I have done something wrong is to say,

"That's just the way I am, deal with it.";
"I can't help it"
"It was just an impulsive act; you know what I am like."

Once again this statement is a denial of the gravity of my poor behaviour. Instead I am suggesting it is normal for me but what this statement does is shift the footing of your attack. I make it appear that you are no longer attacking the act or the event but you are actually assaulting me as a whole. You are cutting me down. With a deft move to Projection I am able to reinforce my denial.

If you are getting a bit smart and provide me with some evidence of my wrongdoing, for example a text or a recording, I will claim it is out of context. If that is not working, I will then deny the standpoint you are doing. Yes, you might very well have caught me flirting with our neighbour again and you have filmed it and played it back to me, but there is nothing wrong with me talking to someone is there? I cannot deny the act but I can deny the connotation you attach to it. After all, one person's flirting is another person's friendliness surely?

My final act of denial is just to walk away. I am no longer even admitting that the conversation is happening and thus I can deny its contents. The step of walking off and making myself unavailable is a two-pronged denial move. It is a powerful and in effect a cut-off of the conversation. My denial is so great I can just leave. It also denies you any further opportunity to continue to harangue me. I deny the issue and you are denied the chance to air the issue.

Ultimately, however, you face one huge problem. My use of denial is set in stone and will always be used and cannot be defeated. There is a straightforward reason for this. In my mind I always minimise the impact of what I have done. I trivialise it and regard it as de minimis. I then rationalise that what I did was actually required and was justified. Since I deny to myself that I have done anything wrong, how on earth can I ever admit it to you? My denials to you are predicated on my internal denial to myself. That is why I can keep denying and denying and denying. You are dealing with an immovable force. The use of denial is a lynchpin in maintaining the avoidance of accountability and thus preserving the fifth narcissistic pillar.

6.6 Blame Shifting

The sixth narcissistic pillar is blame shifting. This is a crucial element to our make up. Once again you will note that this pillar is linked to the others. We are able to shift the blame onto other people by reason of our elevated position (status), by reason of our power (omnipotence), because we can do what we want (entitlement), we are better than you and thus can point the finger because you are inferior (superiority) and we are not responsible (lack of accountability). This pillar sits close to the pillar of a lack of accountability but there is a distinct difference between the two. With a lack of accountability, we are not to blame. With blame shifting it is your fault. When we exert a lack of accountability we may not assert that someone else is to blame, we instead deny and reject any assertion that it is we. When we blame-shift we use this pillar and central part of our make-up to put the blame on someone else and that someone else is usually you.

The main method by which we blame shift is through projection. Everybody projects although most people do it unwittingly and with no real consequence. My kind and me do it intentionally and we do so for a multiplicity of reasons.

What is happening here is that I see my own unacceptable behaviour and desires in other people. I put that behaviour there so it no longer becomes my behaviour and desire but I see them as belonging to someone else and thus I am absolved of any responsibility for them. I also do this so I can feel superior. You have the unpleasant behaviour, not me and accordingly, I am superior to you. Once again the pillars are linked.

Projection serves both as a defence mechanism for me and a method of control concerning you. I know the awful behaviours I engage in and I also am fully aware of my real, damaged self. This terrible reality slams into me either as a consequence of you telling me the truth of what I have done or periodically I have a terrifying moment of self-realisation and it hurts. This usually stems from criticism, which I hate. This is when real damage is done to me and I have to use my ignited fury to defend myself.

The pain I feel when I am given a dose of this reality from time to time is overwhelming. Rather than try to change how I behave so this pain might be relieved or be permanently erased, I need something to provide me with a quick fix to get rid of it. The answer is projection. I immediately accuse you of the very thing I am or the very thing that I have done. You are the dishonest one, you are telling lies, you do not show any consideration towards me and you are the one chasing other people outside of our relationship. It is you that forgot the correct birthday present or you messed up the work presentation. I am wired to do this projection automatically. I often do it without thinking and I truly believe what I am saying is correct. I have to be convinced of this for it to work.

Whether it has been triggered by your comment to me or a sliver of self-realisation, I have to remove the agony I feel rapidly. Therefore, you are told that you are the problem, you are hysterical and you are selfish. I immediately feel relieved of the behaviour and the pain vanishes (but only for now).

This is also done to afford me control of you. By projecting my behaviour onto you, I am reinforcing that you have low self-esteem. I must reinforce that message to you and thus this gives me greater control over you. Attacking you in this fashion enables me to shift from feeling hurt and in pain to feeling empowered once again. That is why projection is so useful to me and why it happens automatically.

The sheer scale of my accusations against you when it is blatantly obvious that I am the one in the wrong will leave you stunned. I will always engage in this behaviour. If in court the judge criticises me for not copying in my opponent and say an independent expert with a piece of correspondence or a witness statement. I will project. I should have copied them in, but I am being criticised and therefore I will retort by stating,

"I don't receive copies of documents from them."

There is absolutely no basis in this comment. They have always copied me in. Someone healthy might respond by saying,

"I am sorry I forgot" or "I didn't realise I had to, I will do it next time."

I will not. I immediately project my failing by accusing the other party in the case and the expert of doing the very thing I have not done even though it is a complete fabrication. It is an aggressive default setting. I am a projection machine such is the immediacy and regularity by which I utilise this technique.

The deployment of this tactic is also particularly wearing for you. You will tire of hearing me trot out the same responses (because you have to keep pointing out to me the same transgressions that I repeat time and time again). This will, like many of my manipulative techniques wear you down so that in the end you will cease to argue with me about it. You are then handing me control by validating the behaviour by no longer criticising it. This is why blame shifting is at the very heart of what we are because it provides us with both a method of defence and attack.

You will probably be aware enough to realise that I am labelling you with the horrible actions that I commit although you will not have realised that I am projecting onto you. Instead, you will be flabbergasted by the rank hypocrisy that I am exhibiting. I know I am being a hypocrite and I am doing it on purpose. In part is for the reasons detailed above but it is also because I know you are aware I am being a hypocrite and I want to provoke a reaction from you. You will find it very hard not to react to the appearance of my hypocrisy as you will see it as a shot at an open goal You will be surprised that I have left myself wide open to such an opportunity. What you do not know is that I have done this on purpose and done this so that you will react and react strongly. This will give me more attention and thus more fuel. It is also likely to cause you to erupt and therefore I can label you as histrionic, unstable and crazy. This provides me with some useful materials to use in other forms of manipulation.

Blame shifting enables me to achieve several things: -

- A method of defence from your attacks against me and rejecting criticism
- A method of control by asserting that I am in the right and you are wrong
- A further method of wearing you down by projecting the blame on to you which is something you cannot understand yet you will keep trying to make me see the incorrect nature of what I am doing, to no avail
- Provocation so that you react and provide me with that all-important fuel.

Thus the sixth narcissistic pillar is that of blame shifting and as described it is an important element of our existence.

6.7 Attention Seeking

The seventh pillar concerns our insatiable desire for attention because as you know well by know your attention and that of other people when combined with some form of emotion becomes fuel for us. Accordingly, we need to attract our attention. Attention also draws people to us, which in turn provides us with the opportunity to attract those people we regard as appropriate to our station and status. We regard ourselves with such importance that we want to ensure we engage with the brilliant and the best. This means that we need to gain their attention and in doing so we can then pull those precious shards and segments from them to create the construct that is so important to our existence.

By being known to fraternise with a group of academics this then demonstrates that we are of similar intellectual excellence. We draw from them the very thing we want other observers to regard as what we actually are. At work we ensure we catch the eye of the higher-ups so that our subordinates see that we are material within the business and clearly on the up. By spending time with gym bunnies we too are able to portray an image of being focused on our physical appearance. Since we are with those who exhibit athletic excellence we must also be of a similar ilk. In all of these grouping we do two things. Our association creates an image that we are similar to them. By being seen with success we must naturally be successful in our own right. Furthermore, we are able to extract from these individuals, information about their own achievements and then pass them off as our own when dealing with people from outside of this group. We are extremely capable of picking up these fragments and titbits and then convincingly applying them to ourselves. To do this we must gain the attention of these people so that they provide us with fuel but also to allow us to extract these segments and shards for our further use.

We will appear as a successful individual who is contemplating making a donation to a university. With such a pretext we have gained the attention of the academics who make us feel welcome so that we are invited to the next university event and sit at the top table. This will then form the basis of our boasts to those at work to exhibit our academic credentials. "Of course one can only be invited if one is of sufficient academic achievement oneself," I will tell those listening. The higher-ups will be impressed by my involvement and this will not only give me fuel but also allow me to spend further time with them as they welcome someone into their fold who is clearly going places. Gaining their confidence and attention I thus acquire information which I can use against the subordinates or perhaps to induce a supplier to do me a favour, let's say organise my attendance in a corporate box at the next home match. I meet numerous people in that box and I am seen on the balcony by others at the match who notice whom I am with. Steadily by moving from group to group and gaining their attention I am extracting parts for the construct, gathering fuel and increasing my status.

This will then provide me with plenty of material to show off in front of those who may regard themselves as my peers, but also sub-ordinates, friends, family and minions. They will be impressed and in turn I gain their attention by mentioning whom I was with at the football match, the famous person I am playing a round of golf with and such like. This gives me fuel from the admiring comments and looks and keeps the attention focussed on me.

Attention is a key part of our existence. It is a component in the provision of fuel and it is also the modus operandi by which we can gather those shards and sections to create our construct.

Attention seeking is naturally connected to the other pillars. By reason of how special I am you will give me attention (status), I expect your attention (entitlement) and someone as powerful as I is bound to attract your attention (omnipotence). By reason of my elevated position and your inferiority to me you give me attention (superiority) and my behaviour in throwing off the yokel of responsibility allows attracts your attention (lack of accountability). My capacity for projection on others always results in you giving me attention, usually of an angry and exasperated nature (blame-shifting). Thus you can see how once more the pillars are all connected to one another and thus support one another.

My attention seeking manifests in a number of ways: -

- Boasting
- Showing off
- Usurping other people, for example at birthdays and at Christmas
- Feigning illness
- Causing a scene
- Requiring you to attend on me by cooking, cleaning etc for me
- Grand gestures
- Exhibiting largesse
- Tantrums
- Silent treatment and other manipulative behaviour designed to gain your attention

If I do not gain attention from you, from him or from her. If I do not have the spotlight on me or I am not centre stage. If I do not have all eyes in my direction or I do not have you worshipping me then I do not have a key component for the extraction of fuel. Fuel is attention plus emotional reaction. I can gather attention but it must also come with the emotional reaction otherwise it is no good to me. I must have attention to continue my work in taking the traits from others and applying them to myself.

Accordingly, attention is a most important constituent element of my very being and something that you will need to target, as I will detail in the following chapter.

6.8 Lack of Empathy

And so we reach the eighth and final narcissistic pillar, our famed lack of empathy. In the same way that we have not been created to feel guilt, remorse or a need to care, we have no ability to feel empathy. As I have written previously we know what empathy looks like because we see our victims exhibit it repeatedly. We are masters of studying so we see how you show empathy and we can easily do the same. Accordingly, during the period of seduction we are able to show you what you think is sympathy when you talk about how badly hurt you have been by your ex partner. We can show sadness and make the right noises when something upsetting occurs to you during the seduction. We feel nothing. We feel no need to support you, we feel no sympathy, we feel no kinship and we feel no empathy. We display it purely to achieve our own agendas. We want you to think that we are kind, caring and empathic. We want you to open up to us as you tell us all about your weaknesses and vulnerabilities so that we can file them away for later use against you. We want to create this impression of being someone who is compassionate and cares all in order to bind you closer to us.

Once devaluation occurs you will soon realise that we have no empathy whatsoever. It usually first manifests when you ask for our support when you suffer some kind of setback, a difficult day at work, illness or a disagreement with a friend. We have no interest in showing this faux empathy to you now because we have already managed to seduce you. To continue to portray ourselves as empathic uses up energy which is better applied to gathering fuel. Indeed, our lack of empathy provokes upset in you, which is naturally good fuel. As time progresses you realises that whenever there is a crisis and you need someone who understands your situation, someone to put an arm around you and empathise with the upset and pain that you are going through, that we go missing. Death in the family? We vanish. Lost your job? Nowhere to be seen. Sister found out she has cancer? Absent. You are left to struggle on alone. If we remained, we would get no fuel because the attention is on you and your travails. It is not on me. You might have thanked me for helping you and those words of appreciation do not provide me with fuel because your attention will be on yourself or your sick relative or grieving mother and not us, thus the component of attention, as I have explained above, is missing and thus we are denied our fuel. Being with you on such an occasion has no value to us. Indeed, if we were to be there and have to comfort you, we would be using up our energy whilst not receiving any fuel and this would trouble us.

When you do eventually find us and look to remonstrate with us for not being there we will drink this fuel that you now provide. Your attention is on us for having gone missing and your anger and upset provides the emotional reaction to create the fuel we need. We will deny we have done anything wrong and look to deflect your criticism of us. If you mention that you have lost your job, we will bring it back to being about us and point out how we once lost a job but we got on with it and did not cause a song and dance. None of that may be true but we will still say it in order to take attention off your woes and being the attention firmly back to us.

If you are ill, we will not nurse you. We will either make ourselves scarce or if that is not possible we will spend our time pointing out that you are not that ill and bemoaning the fact you have not done the laundry or made our dinner for us. You will be staggered by this selfishness but to us it is an entirely appropriate reaction. We cannot feel any empathy for you, we have no need to fabricate it and everything must be about us in order to provide us with the fuel we need. By being created so that we do not feel empathy we have been divested of this huge hindrance. Consider how your empathic nature impacts on you? You will not mind of course because it is a core trait of yours and something, which you take great pride in but when you display empathy this may mean you have to take time off work to care for someone, cancel arrangements and not do the things you had planned to do. You do not mind but it prevents you from doing what you may want to do. We cannot tolerate such a situation. We cannot be hindered in this way. We must be direct, sleek and fleet of foot. We must move rapidly, unencumbered by unnecessary emotions so we can stalk our prey and sink our fangs into them to draw deep on their fuel. If we felt empathy, we would be slowed down and most of all we would end up questioning our own behaviour in light of this empathy. We know it to be wrong but we do not feel it to be wrong because we do not feel empathy. If we started to feel empathy, then we would not go after our victims in the way we do. We would not roll out the manipulative devices since once we saw them upset we would empathise and look to do something to make everything well again. We would be denied our fuel and thus the construct would begin to collapse and eventually, devoid of fuel, we would cease to exist. Thus, for this very good reason we have been created so we do not feel empathy. This in turn means that a lack of empathy is at our very core and is the final narcissistic pillar.

7.   Toppling the Narcissistic Pillars

So, now you are armed with the requisite knowledge to allow you to commence the practical side of your revenge campaign. You have read and understood the theory. You know what seeking revenge entails and you have established that it is appropriate to your circumstances. You understand the Core Principle and how it must be applied in the course of seeking revenge. You have grasped the ultimate aim. You know what type of narcissist you are dealing with and therefore you are better placed to understand what to expect by way of response and the extent of the task that lies before you. The targets by way of the narcissistic pillars have been revealed to you and you recognise each one. You comprehend how they are linked and you understand the behaviours and traits associated with each one. You know that these are your targets and this is where your energies must be applied in the application of your revenge. Now you are ready to read what practical steps can be taken to topple each of these pillars and having done so you will achieve the ultimate aim and destroy the narcissist.

Before I begin with demonstrating to you what steps you can take, I will return to the issue of the type of narcissist you are dealing with and how many pillars support their existence. I earlier detailed the number. You may have established in your own mind which pillars apply to which narcissist but by way of confirmation I set this out below.

Category	Number	Type of Pillar
Lesser Victim Narcissist	Five pillars	Ent, LofA,Blame, LofE, Att
Mid-Range Victim Narcissist	Six pillars	as above plus superiority
Mid-Range Cerebral Narcissist	Six pillars	Ditto
Greater Cerebral Narcissist	Eight pillars	All
Mid-range Somatic Narcissist	Seven pillars	All save Omnipotence
Greater Somatic Narcissist	Eight pillars	All
Mid-range Elite Narcissist	Seven pillars	All save Omnipotence
Greater Elite Narcissist	Eight pillars	All

Now you can identify which pillars you will need to attack and how many. Naturally, some of you will face a tougher task than others. Now we turn to how you should go about attacking each of the pillars through the application of practical techniques. Remember, this must all be done in accordance with the Core Principle.

7.1 Toppling the Status Pillar

It is worth mentioning before we tackle the ways by which you can attack this narcissistic pillar that you do not have to attack the pillars in sequence. You can choose any of the pillars when you commence your assault. You can look to attack several at once, move your attack from one to another. There is not set pattern. Since they are connected, an attack on one will not only weaken that pillar and eventually topple it but this will also affect the strength of the other pillars as well. In orchestrating your attacks on these pillars it will be of considerable assistance if you are able to call on help from your support networks. Naturally, those people need to be people whom your trust but through the period of No Contact you most likely will have been able to establish who you could trust and rely on. Furthermore, over the period my Lieutenants will have withdrawn owing to the success of your No Contact and therefore you may well have been able to identify them.

What steps should you take to topple the status pillar? You will need to have regard as well to the last chapter in terms of steps you should not take before commencing these attacks, but once done, here are the things you should be looking to do. Keep in mind where I advocate sending us anything you should do so in a manner, which protects your contact details if you have managed to change them and keep them from us. Do not open up the risk of having us contact you by mistakenly providing a new address or a new e-mail address. Use a temporary account or enlist the help of your support network.

Organise for letters to be sent by you and your support network to us at our place of work. The letters should be addressed to using the wrong job title and preferably with one, which is regarded as being of a lesser status. For example, if we hold the position of say Sales Director within an organisation, have the letter addressed to Mr A Narcissist, Washroom Attendant, ABC Inc. You can enjoy thinking up all manner of lesser titles such as Chief Photocopier or Head of Watercooler Logistics and even ridiculous ones for instance Executive Foliage Numerator (a leaf counter) Assistant Footstool or Deputy Brown Noser. Using words such as Deputy, Assistant, Under or Acting are useful as this denotes an even lesser role by being someone who is only able to step in when the main person is absent. There is no need to include addresses with your letters. You may wish to let the narcissist know the letter is from you, as this will infuriate us all the more. The content of the letter must be neutral and I would suggest something along the lines of

"I am writing in recognition of your ten-year tenure as Apprentice Toilet Roll Dispenser."

There is no emotion in this correspondence, the letters get our status wrong but even worse they suggest we hold a lesser position than the one we are in. This will be a criticism to us. There is also the possibility of other people seeing the letters, which may subject us to additional ridicule.

Organise for telephone calls to be made to our secretary or a colleague explaining you are calling from XYZ Corporation and just wanted to let Mr A Narcissist know that his application for the position of (insert details of lowly position) has been successful and we will be in touch to discuss a start date. This message will invariably be relayed to us.

If you know our work e-mail address use it to subscribe to updates and information from certain recruitment sites which cater for a sector beneath that which we are in. Receiving repeated reminders about catering assistant positions or super market checkout operators will irritate us.

During your time with us you may be aware of certain actions we took at work, which would could potentially expose us to dismissal. If you have such information you should present it to the organisation. Do not threaten us with taking such a step and do not fabricate any such information. If you are aware that for instance we have bullied staff, fiddled expenses, stolen stock etc then report it to the organisation and let them investigate it. You can do so anonymously and most organisations will at least look into it. If you can provide evidence of the wrongdoing all the better. Do not follow up by asking the organisation what is happening, they are unlikely to tell you, but after a suitable period of time you can contact the organisation to find out if A. Narcissist is still working there and if not you know your work has succeeded in causing him to resign or be dismissed. Once the removal has been achieved send a neutral note to the narcissist along the lines of "I see you no longer work at ABC Inc. Justice." The loss of the position through having our unacceptable workplace behaviour exposed will cause us considerable loss of status. Naturally if you are reliant on us for money (that is if somehow you have compelled us to pay) say through child support then you do not want to take this option. Always leave it to the organisation to investigate and take action. This allows the step to be taken in a manner, which is emotion free and moreover in accordance with the relevant law. Once you know removal has occurred you can then deliver an emotion free comment telling the narcissist you know what has happened and inferring you caused it.

A similar approach should be used if you are aware of misconduct on our part (and more so if you can prove it) in respect of our membership of certain clubs, organisation and committees. Causing our expulsion from these will prove very satisfying for you and most damaging for us.

Organise for invitations to be sent to us for minor events, which you know we will regard as beneath us. Place us on the mailing list for certain organisations, which you know we hold in contempt. Receiving flyers and invitations to these organisations will cause us further irritation and annoyance as we are clearly above them and we will be infuriated that someone is contacting us from these organisations.

If you have retained any expensive gifts that we may have given you, no doubt you will recall the numerous occasions we will have made mention of this in order to exhibit our generosity and largesse. These reminders were also issued to demonstrate status. You are regarded as an extension of us and by providing you with expensive clothes, perfume, jeweller, household products and such like, we are reminding ourselves of our elevated status. As I have explained in **Escape: How to Beat the Narcissist** you need to remove these items as they amount to Ever Presence. I recommend three different ways of effecting this removal, which will strike hammer blows against our sense of status.

Firstly, you may decide you may as well benefit from the value of these items and therefore you wish to sell them. If you have placed classified advertisements for the items so they are readily identifiable as something that has come from us, then you should send a copy of the advertisement to us. I recommend in the advertisement you use the phrase "Unwanted gift". The fact you are selling the item will be abhorrent to us. Alternatively sell the items on e-bay and send the links to us. We will easily recognise the items and be devastated at you selling them, partially because this removes Ever Presence but mainly as you are attacking our sense of status.

Secondly you may decide to give the items away for free. If you do so and have placed an advertisement again send it to us. Even better would be getting a friend to film you taking a box of the items and handing them over to a charity shop explaining "I do not want them as they mean nothing to me, so I thought other people could make use of them. No I do not want anything for them." Then organise for this footage to be sent to me. Ensure your handover is done without rancour or delight, just remain neutral. The fact you have given away items, which we paid for, will feel like you have walked in our own house and began giving away our own possessions for nothing. It will infuriate us and damage our sense of status.

The third step is where you decide destruction of the items is most appropriate. A fire is always a good way of doing this. Again have this filmed and present each item to the camera before saying,

"I have no need of this worthless item. I am deleting it like I have deleted you." As ever speak in a neutral, business like fashion and then consign the item to the flames before selecting whatever it is next. We will watch with horror and a growing sense of weakness as we see each item being presented to us, described as worthless and then ignored as you have ignored us by deleting us before it is dropped into the flames. Place the item in the flames, do not hurl it. Act like you are putting rubbish in the bin. Each time you do this you will be driving a blow against us. Then arrange for the footage to be sent to us.

In the second and third instances upload the video to youtube. Do not make any mention of the name of your narcissist but entitle the video along the lines of "Deleting the narcissist." Knowing the world can see these status symbols being destroyed or given away will drive a hammer blow against us. Even though nobody will know who we are this will not matter because we believe we are better known and more famous than we actually are. The fact you have even omitted to name us will wound further. No emotion is provided in the making of the video or its posting and thus we cannot derive fuel from it. Instead you are landing sledgehammer blows against our status pillar.

Should our property go by a name rather than a number arrange for correspondence to be sent to it utilising another name in the address. Address it to "The Frozen Wasteland" or "The Torture Chamber" or "Weakling Towers" or something similar. The correspondence need not be from you but if it is it will be all the more damning. The letter inside can be blank with just your name or the letters can come from your support group. You could sign up to mailing lists using such an address. The effect of having our castle, our place referred to in a derogatory fashion without the accompanying emotion will wound us. Each time we pick up a catalogue or one of the letters and see it addressed to "Mr A Narcissist, Impotent Ruins" you will land a further blow against us.

If you have any of your support network who you can rely on who are in a position to effect the following you should ensure that they do so on your behalf: -

- Seating us at a poor table in a restaurant

- Failing to serve us in a timely manner in a bar or restaurant;

- Deny us access to an event

- Miss us off invitations to parties, dinner parties, drinks receptions and the like

- Remove us from waiting lists for tickets for special events

- Downgrade our seating at events

Admittedly you may not have access to such people but where you do and you know that you can rely on them to do this with little risk that they will face repercussions from such actions then you should ask them to assist you in this regard. Again since they will be delivered by a third party and not you, we will not get fuel from them from you. By coaching the member of your support network to act in a firm and polite manner, without expressing annoyance or pleasure at denying what we want you will also be preventing us from gaining fuel from the third party as well.

If you know we delight in flashing a black or Platinum American Express card around, arrange for invitations for high interest credit cards to be sent to us, the type that people with poor credit are obliged to us. The inference will not be lost on us when these mail shots keep landing on the mat.

You should look to have us ousted from any committees we may sit on, from the Parent Teachers' Association to charitable trustees and the like. If you have evidence of wrongdoing, then place it in the appropriate hands and leave them to get on with it. In other instances, consider persuading someone you can rely on to run in opposition to us in the hope of securing the position over you. You can be conspicuous in supporting this friend but remain neutral in your dealings with us. By bringing about our removal from committees and the like, either through disciplinary means or loss of elected office you will again be striking at our status.

If you know of discussion groups, forums and the like where our achievements are referred to then arrange for negative postings to be made about the publication or achievement by you and others. The observation should be short and without an explanation, which can be challenged, it is just an expression of opinion and one, which you are perfectly entitled to have. For example, should there be a review site of a particular paper delivered by us then you may wish to write

"This is not very good."

You need not add anymore. There is no emotion in this statement and it is a clear criticism. We frequently check on comments about our works and seeing a string of one-liners in this manner will amount to criticism and cause us damage.

There is in all likelihood the significant likelihood that we have put in place a new primary source of fuel. This individual will be of a trophy nature to us. This person will be paraded as something for people to be envious of. Keep in mind that approaching the new primary source of fuel is always a risk because you WILL have been labelled as the troublemaker and the crazy one. If you are able to either yourself or even better using a third party, approach the new source when he or she is not with their narcissist and explain in a matter of fact way,

"You are at risk of being abused."

The show them clear evidence of abusive behaviour towards you. A video recording would be best and the more instances the better. Do not seek to persuade this person that is too much. Do not speak with anger or delight, remain business like. Although you are not dealing with us direct, this approach will be brought to our attention. Answer any questions the primary source may have and remain business like. Your role or that of the third party is not to make the decision for them but allow them to see the evidence and reach their own conclusion. By adopting this evidence-based approach, which is devoid of emotion, you have two bites at the cherry. Firstly, the new primary source of fuel will in most instances report this approach to us. This is because they will want to know our reaction. We will feel our status under attack by the manner in which you have approached our trophy. You have sought to remove our trophy and in a non-fuel method. This will sting. Even if we manage to persuade him or her to stay, you will have inflicted damage.

Secondly, your approach may work and the primary source of fuel will leave. Not only have you caused us a massive problem by removing our primary source of fuel without us having another lined up, you have driven a considerable blow against our status. This is a difficult step to pull off, mainly owing to your labelling as the crazy one and the fact that we will indoctrinate the primary fuel source and be in a full on golden period. Even if you fail to cause their departure you will have landed a blow anyway by attacking our trophy in an emotion free manner.

If you know of any achievements we say we have, check with the relevant body whether that is true and if it is not ask for this in writing and then send a copy to us and to other people who know us. The dissemination of this information in an emotion free manner will strike yet another blow against our status. If we have acquired the achievement in fraudulent circumstances and you have evidence to counter this, use it and allow the relevant investigating body to reach its own conclusion. Even if the outcome is not as you would want any situation where our status is called into question by our work, our bank, our club, a committee, an awarding body and so on will be an attack against our status. It may not result in dismissal or the stripping of an achievement (although sometimes it will) but the fact we have been exposed to an investigation by people who will treat us in a neutral fashion will damage our sense of status. Our paranoid nature will always ensure that we believe you (and other former intimate partners) to be behind such actions so you need not always be concerned about ensuring that we know who has taken such steps.

Contact an estate agent or realtor and explain that you are away on business but need a drive-by valuation of your (our) property on the basis of a quick sale as we need access to funds. Explain that the valuation should be posted to us and we will then contact you to arrange an internal viewing to fine tune the valuation. Chances are that by virtue of being a drive-by valuation and with reference to a fire sale the valuation will be depressed. When we open the letter and read that the property has been valued far less than we believe it should be valued at this will land a further blow against our status pillar.

You will notice that many of these steps rely on indirect communications through post and electronically. This and the content of the communication ensure that there is no emotion attached and therefore we are not provided with any fuel. It also allows you to achieve repeated and frequent assaults on our status through many e-mails, letters and such like. These will be like rapid machine gun bullets peppering our status as your campaign to achieve revenge progresses. By adopting such techniques and applying them repeatedly you are denying us any fuel through your actions and causing us repeated criticism. Our fury will be ignited but in some instances we will not know where to direct it or be unable to do so because you have remained at arms' length. There is every chance we will lash out at you as our fury erupts. If this is the case maintain the principles of No Contact so that this lashing out draws no fuel. We are unable to withdraw because your assaults are targeting us at our home and work and we are left with really nowhere to go to evade them. Instead we will be forced to use our power to shield ourselves from these repeated criticisms. This will drain our reserves of fuel, you are no providing us with any and we will weaken. I cannot give you an exact period over which you will have to keep maintaining these steps before you achieve revenge. It will depend on factors such as: -

- The frequency of the attacks. If they are daily you are preventing us from recovering from them, as our fuel will be used to shield us from them.

- The nature of the narcissist. A greater narcissist takes more toppling by reason of having more pillars but also because we will put up more of a fight to defend ourselves and we have more resources at our disposal.

- Whether you are attacking other pillars at the same time as attacking the status pillar

By applying a combination of the above techniques on a daily basis you will bring about the collapse of the status tower within a few weeks, possibly less.

7.2 Toppling the Entitlement Pillar

Next comes the second narcissistic pillar, the Pillar of Entitlement. The following steps can be used to bring this pillar down.

Our sense of entitlement means that we believe we are entitled to belong to the best clubs, sit on certain committees and belong to exclusive organisations. In the same way you attacked our status with reference to clubs and committees you will also be inflicting damage on the entitlement pillar when you attach the status pillar in respect of these things. You will be achieving a double whammy.

We frequently pass judgement on people and their lives, which are borne out of our sense of entitlement. You should coach and advise those who have contact with us to learn to respond when placed on the receiving end of such judgements with a simple comment,

"Your opinion is not valid."

Nothing more needs to be said. The lack of explanation and it being delivered in a business-like and emotion free manner will cause us consternation and also prevent us from gathering fuel. Thus a successful attack will have been launched. By denying the validity of our opinion you are challenging our entitlement to do as we please. If you have contact with us, you will be able to say this although of course you will be exposing yourself to a potential Hoover. You should be in a position to resist it given your increased strength, respite following No Contact and determination to achieve revenge. A useful way of attacking our judgemental behaviour is to do the following: -

- Set up an e-mail account through one of the providers such as notvalid@yahoo.com or judgement@gmail.com

- Use this account to send e-mails to our e-mail addresses

- The e-mails should refer to judgemental behaviour you have been made aware of that we have engaged in and state such things like
    "Your comments about John Smith's car are not valid."
    "Your opinion about Jane Smith and her family is not valid."

- If we respond just repeat the message

By doing this you are not granting us fuel but you are challenging us and doing so in a manner which gives us very little to attack. We may answer stating why our view is valid but just answer in the same way. Keep repeating it every time we state something and you learn about it and every time we respond to your e-mail. It is matter of fact, devoid of emotion and it will torture us to have someone dismiss us in such a way and deny our sense of entitlement to pass judgement on others. You are criticising us by denying the validity of what we say without even providing a reason for it (the type of thing that we would do) and it wounds us to be subjected to this.

If you are able to exert influence over anybody who is in a position to generate delay for us, make us wait or force us to queue you should avail yourself of the opportunity to do so. Being made to wait drives us up the wall because you are denying our entitlement to do what we want and be masters of our own fate. If you know the owner of the local garage where our car is serviced see if he will do you a favour and delay the work on our vehicle. If a friend works at or owns a restaurant, ask them to engineer a longer wait than usual when we turn up at the restaurant. If we do our usual trick and expect to be seated without reservations, ask that we be turned away.

If we owe you money take steps to recover it. Place the recovery in the hands of a friend or if you can afford to do so a lawyer or debt recovery outfit. Using a third party removes the prospect of us obtaining fuel. We will twist and squirm to avoid payment but ultimately if it is owed you should be able to prove it and recover it. Forcing us to pay for things when we believe we are entitled to walk away from payment lands another blow against us. If possible organise for a debt collection agency to make a call to us every day at home and at work, pressing for payment. This daily reminder of your desire for recovery through a medium, which will not provide us with fuel, will keep landing repeated blows against us.

If we have property, which belongs to, you send someone to collect it or hire a lawyer to secure its return. Having two burly fellows on our doorstep politely requesting the return of the items in a business like manner will drive another blow against our sense of entitlement. We may refuse and look to wriggle out of returning the item but the fact of being challenged in a non-fuel manner will damage us. We want you to turn up shouting and shrieking and demanding the return of the relevant item. When somebody unrelated to you and I arrive asking for it, we gain no fuel and it makes us feel weak. We may, especially if you are landing other blows against this pillar (and also other pillars) be weakening so that we give up the item. This will hurt us further and of course give you additional delight at having secured the return of the item.

A significant way of landing a hammer blow against the pillar of entitlement is to exert your right to privacy. You should have begun this when you commenced No Contact by changing passwords, removing yourself from social media, changing telephone numbers, sweeping your home for bugs, checking for tracking devices and so on. Since we do not recognise boundaries we believe we are entitled to all and every piece of information about you. If you maintain a neat impenetrable wall and in so doing assert your right to privacy you will strike a considerable blow against us. You can also take this step further by invading our privacy and thus our entitlement is hit again. You can do this by arranging for marketing companies to keep calling us to ask us questions but about things which are completely irrelevant to us such as stair lift products and the like. If it is something that we are happy to answer questions about then this attention along with the overtures from the marketer or research individual will give us fuel. Having somebody ring up and ask us about our interest in a speedboat when we live miles from open water will irritate us especially when it impinges on our privacy.

Look to have the rules applied to us. If you know we have not paid parking fines, then inform the relevant authority. If you are aware we under state our income, notify the revenue. You will have plenty of information on us, which evidences our flagrant disregard for the rules, which is linked to our sense of entitlement, because we will like to boast about. Never report us for something, which is untrue as you are scoring an own goal but where you know and especially if you can provide evidence of our failure to adhere to rules and regulations then you should report us. Such examples might include: -

- A failure to obtain planning permission for home improvements;

- The absence of a licence which is required in a certain profession or occupation

- Traffic offences

- Criminal acts

- Fly tipping

- Breaches of health and safety and food hygiene

- Failure to pay housing rates or claiming exemptions when not entitled to do so

Any instance where you can bring about at the very least some form of investigation and even better a sanction so that we are reminded that our sense of entitlement does not allow us to do as we please, will be causing a blow to be landed against our entitlement pillar.

If you are in a position to do so yourself or call in favours from others to effect this make sure we are made to jump through all the hoops if we are applying for something. We expect to go straight to the top and cut through what everyone else must do. If you are in a position to make us fill in forms, wait, provide evidence in support of an application, and attend courses and such like then you should avail yourself of such an opportunity.

Re-establish and reinforce barriers and invite those of your supporters to do the same with us. Have friends tell us that our flirting is not welcome. Have family point out to us that they cannot be expected to child mind at a moment's notice. If you are in a situation where there is contact between us and we are behaving in a manner, which transgresses your personal space, then you should tell us so in a neutral fashion,

"You are invading my space. You are not allowed to do that."

This again attacks our sense of entitlement. If we keep hanging around your property involve the police rather than confront us yourself. The principles applied during No Contact are useful here as you exert your own boundaries and reject our overtures as well.

Our sense of entitlement causes us to always believe that we are right. If you can engineer a situation at a dinner party or even better where we might be giving a speech or leading some kind of lecture or workshop arrange for someone more erudite than us to attend so that when we begin to hold forth on a subject this person is in prime position to cut us down with fact after fact after fact. If you are in attendance as well the impact will be increased. You need not say anything. In fact, remain implacable as we flail and flounder seeking to fight back against someone more expert than us. We will know you are behind it and this criticism of our entitlement to hold our opinions and espouse our expertise will damage our entitlement pillar further.

7.3 Toppling the Pillar of Omnipotence

This third pillar, the one, which demonstrates our power and our magnificence, affords you many opportunities to land telling blows against us. The key to attacking this pillar is to be aware that there are principally two limbs which can used. The first is to remind us of our mortality to dispel our notions of god-like grandeur. The second is to diminish and extinguish the powers we purport to wield.

Dealing with this first limb, the attack needs to be both as a whole and specific to the senses. Anything which reminds us that we are growing older and infirmity awaits is a substantial blow against our omnipotence. The prospect of aging, our strength dwindling as our senses become dim and muted, our physicality diminishing and our mental faculties blunted, fills us with horror. We do not wish to contemplate the sagging of our skin, the multitude of lines, the receding the hairline and the broken and rotten teeth. We do no want to be reminded that our bladders will weaken, our memories will cloud, that our mental sharpness will lessen and our thoughts will become fuddled. The prospect of amnesia and dementia are twin terrors that lurk ready to steal from us our intellectual superiority. Greater Somatic, cerebral and especially elite narcissists dread the onset of age and its complications. It is no great concern to the mid-range as omnipotence does not form one of their pillars and as for the lesser victim narcissist he will welcome age and infirmity as further excuses and reasons to have his particular empathic individual mother him all the more.

In order to strike this pillar down using the first limb of attack you need to take steps, as ever devoid of emotion, in order to remind us of the encroaching feebleness that awaits us. To this end, you should take the following steps: -

- Organise for flyers, mail and appointments to be sent to us concerning hearing aids

- Organise for people to speak in a slower and louder fashion when near us and for them to lean into us. If we query this ensure people explain that they understood our hearing was being lost

- If you are in contact with us, you may revel (although of course you must not show it) in applying some reverse gas lighting. Should you have occasion to speak to us do so in a loud voice and if we ask why you are doing that, respond and say "Doing what?" If we point out that you are speaking loudly, with a neutral expression state that you are speaking in a normal voice. Later speak in whispers causing us to ask you to repeat yourself. Point out in a polite and business like manner that you are speaking normally and your hearing must be affected. Keep alternating but show no delight in the irritation this causes us.

- Organise optician appointments for us, send us reading glasses and have large print books delivered to us

- Organise dental appointments, have denture products, denture cleaners and fixers sent to us

- Arrange for representatives selling life insurance and funeral plans to make contact with us, put us on their mailing and e-mail circulation lists

- Arrange for us to receive literature dealing with aging, information from age charities, brochures concerning hip replacements, knee replacements, walking aids, meals on wheels and the like

- If your narcissist is a somatic or elite narcissist you may wish to arrange a delivery of viagra with a note "You will need these"

- Leave packets of tablets, which deal with aging complaints such as weak bladders and weak bones in places where we will find them, such as at work, on the bonnet of our vehicle, outside our front door.

- Send information about care and nursing homes, arrange for sales staff from these places to call us

There is a medley of material, which can be used to keep reminding us of the prospect of age and infirmity. You may be wondering whether such a sustained campaign of sending things, arranging calls and adding to mailing lists might amount to harassment. There is potential, dependent on the relevant law of where you live, for this to be the case. I am not in a position to give you any advice as to the law but I can only explain how we will regard it from the narcissist's point of view. There may be a minority of our kind who would act on this sustained campaign and involve law enforcement to make a complaint. Of course, if you have been sensible you will have avoided any way of linking all these steps to you even though we know it is you. However, it is unlikely that we will involve the authorities. There are three reasons for this. We regard ourselves as superior, powerful and impregnable therefore our arrogance will cause us to want to deal with these attacks ourselves (or using our coterie and Lieutenants) but no law enforcement. Secondly, it is likely that our tactics in fighting back will result in a transgression of the law and we do not want to have the law already involved with us when we do so. We will be looking to act undetected. Thirdly and most importantly, we will be weakened by these attacks. Our omnipotence is being challenged (along with the other pillars) and the last thing we want to do is have some police officer smirking as we complain about being sent repeated sets of incontinence pads. Even if they keep a straight face we do not wish to appear weak in front of such people, we do not want to draw attention to this further attack against us and for this reason primarily it is unlikely we will involve law enforcement.

The second limb is to attack our pillar of omnipotence by diminishing and extinguishing our powers. Spreading word about our weaknesses and failings can do this. Some of these will appear innocuous judged by normal people but to us knowing that this is being said about us, that people think this is the case and indeed even go so far to ask us about them means repeated strikes are made against us and this criticism will wound us. Consider for example referring to: -

- The fact we needed to go to the toilet several times a night when we were together;

- That we wore contact lenses but did not want anybody knowing

- We wore reading glasses at home

- We suffered erectile dysfunction

- We have to wear a knee brace when we undertake sport

- We kept forgetting where we had put things

- We could not remember appointments and the like

- Our hair is thinning

Word will soon get back to us but it will not be delivered by you and thus since it will have delivered to us as an inherent criticism of our powerful state we will find ourselves wounded by it.

You also need to consider ways in causing our usual power over people to become weakened. This is best done by explaining to people in a calm and rationale manner, preferably with some form of evidence to hand, what we really are. There will be those who cannot see it and therefore, in the same way as I explained above about dealing with the primary source of fuel, you are not there to cause people to feel they are being forced to think a certain way, but instead you are giving them the facts and letting them decide. Some will reject what you say. Others will not be convinced but will have sufficient doubt to cause them to act with a degree of wariness around us whereas once they were compliant. Others again will agree with you and thus become resistant to the charm and seduction we try to maintain with them, as we want the façade to remain in place. We will of course look to fight back against these attempts to convert others to your way of thinking and thus pull them away from our influence. We will revert to the use of our usual manipulative wiles but if you are exacting this revenge campaign in a measured and sustained fashion, by adhering to the Core Principle you will be weakening us. Our fuel stocks will be diminishing and as all these criticisms ignite our fury, our fuel is being used up to shield us from further attacks whilst trying to repair the damage that has already been inflicted. As more blows land, with fuel in scarce supply and more repair work to undertake we will not have the energy to maintain a charm offensive with others. In addition, these body blows to the narcissistic pillars, which are proving a massive drain on our fuel reserves, mean that the construct will be weakening. Shards and sections will start to crack and fall away.

Consequently, those segments we stole from others to reflect what we want the world to see us as and in turn attract more people to us and thus more fuel, begin to go missing. It becomes a dire situation. We cannot repair the construct fast enough, we are losing sections and shards which mean our capability to gather more fuel through charm, seduction and attraction has been diminished. Deprived of such an ability to gain more fuel and with more blows being dealt to us, our fuel has to be used to protect ourselves rather than gather more. You might liken it to having us on the ropes in boxing. All we can do it keep our gloves up, form a defence and hope for the bell to ring as a means of escape. We are unable to strike back. Usually it is you who is exhausted, depleted and on the back foot but when your revenge campaign is begin effected and you are landing blows against all pillars on a repeated basis, our ability to attack you and gather more fuel from other sources is significantly compromised. We can only hope to hold out until your attack halts and we can then slink away, recuperate, repair the damage and then gather more fuel so we can then go on the attack. Accordingly, the maintenance of your revenge campaign and keeping up a sustained attack is most important.

The omnipotence pillar is once which affords you many options by which you can criticise us and thus bring about the toppling of this pillar. Should you achieve this you will have won a resounding battle with the narcissist in your life as those who have the omnipotence pillar in their make-up are from the greater school.

7.4 Toppling the Pillar of Superiority

Now we near the halfway of the pillars as we look to deal with the pillar of superiority. Like the pillar of omnipotence, there is a two-limbed way of attacking this pillar. You will recall from the previous chapter that our superiority is predicated on two things; your inferiority and our elevation. Thus the approach when attacking this pillar is a dual one. You must remove your inferiority and attack our purported elevation.

Removing your inferiority has several consequences: -

1. You gain strength, which aids you in your campaign;

2. You are rejecting the role which we have assigned to you, thus weakening our control over you; and

3. You are putting yourself on a better footing by which to tackle our supposed elevation.

Your inferiority is embedded in our psyche. We regard you as inferior simply because you must be because you are not us. The traits we regard as weaknesses, the need to care, the display of empathic behaviour, consideration for others, kindness and understanding, the need to comprehend are all things we consider to hinder. Yet, to you they are strengths but we make you think to the contrary. Our vicious campaign of devaluation is based on stripping you of your capabilities by exhausting you but we also get inside your head so that you think less of yourself. We make you think you are inferior. We remove your support networks so that nobody is dissuading you from what we say and nobody is bolstering you.

We take away the things you once enjoyed doing as we strapped you tight to us during the seduction and now when we unleash our vicious vitriol against you, you are left largely alone.

Revitalised from implementing No Contact you will have regained some semblance of which you were before we came along. This is the key to dismantling and toppling our pillar of superiority. You need to remember who you are. You need to remember you are actually strong, clever, talented, beautiful, well-regarded, happy, caring and a hundred other positive traits, which we ground out of you. In order to cast off this mantle of inferiority you must: -

- Make use of your support networks

- Do those things you want to do

- Return to the hobbies you enjoyed

- Seek out new skills and interests

- Return to work (where appropriate)

- Aim for a promotion

- Attend to your physical and mental well being

- Socialise

Your aim is to rise like a phoenix from the flames. Not only must you remove the inferiority you must convey that this is happening to us. Allow photos of you being out to be posted to your friends' social media. We will periodically look. Be seen out and about. Herald your own achievements. If you feel confident of repelling further Hoovers from us now you have recovered your strength you may wish to resurrect those social media accounts and use them to broadcast your return. Just as we revel in an All Points Broadcast Power Play as part of the Grand Hoover this is your chance to exact revenge by announcing your triumphs. This will come to our attention either through the purposeful dissemination of this information by your supporters and/or because we still keep tabs on you. We will be dismayed by the fact that you are asserting yourself. You have thrown off the shackles of our devaluation. Some never do. They may escape us as we go elsewhere and they manage to resist out Hoovers but the damage we do to their self-esteem, identity and personality becomes permanent and this just confirms to us what a pathetic and inferior person he or she way. When you escape us and then make a return to who you were prior to your entanglement with us it not only affects our superiority as you exhibit strengths and scintillating qualities it will also land a blow against our omnipotence as well. We have not disabled you to the extent that we thought we had. You have recovered. You have rose again and therefore we are not as powerful as we thought we were.

In tandem with removing your supposed inferiority you must also attack our inflated ego and our purported superiority. As you rise, you are looking to bring about our fall. Many of your attacks against the pillar of omnipotence will also resonate against superiority. By reminding us we are not the powerful being that we are then you are removing our superiority. You also need to bring about other people regarding us as nothing special. Remember, ordinarily when people try and achieve revenge they do so with emotion and therefore even where they are criticising us it has no effect because we are focussed on gathering the fuel. Furthermore, they are focussed on attacking the wrong things and therefore their blows do very little to injure us. By adopting the approach suggested here you would be landing body blows and thus such rampant criticism, absent the fuel we need, results in us being beaten back. We lose the function to charm others and maintain smear campaigns and character assassinations. This is your chance to seize the opportunity to conduct your own assassinations and turn one of our manipulative tools against us. With our propaganda machine silenced or the volume much turned down you will be able to make others hear you. Have them realise what we have done, that we are not the person we make ourselves out to be, expose our weaknesses, our frauds and our vulnerabilities. As people realise this, supplementary sources of fuel will be removed weakening us further. These people not only will not longer give us admiring attention but they will turn away from us. They will remark about our fraudulent behaviour but in a neutral manner as coached by you. Thus starved of fuel (either positive or negative) we weaken. We may, where we are of a lower function, lash out at these people in order to try and provoke a reaction but this will not now work. They have seen through the curtain. The façade has been pierced. This once magnificent person who showed such largesse, generosity and brilliance was no more than a fraud. Our superiority is cast down, as you not only turn against us but your turn others against us. We are a product of what others regard us to be and once you shatter that illusion, they see we are nowhere near as special and superior was we purported and this will damage us further.

If you have contact with us and we seek to denigrate you, you have learned not to react in the way that you once did. This assertion shows you are not inferiority and further erodes our superiority.

You should also look to undermine and expose our achievements. You may well have done this as part of your assault on the status and/or entitlement pillars and once more this will have a knock on effect against another pillar by affecting the pillar of superiority.

Freed form our controls and manipulations the approach when attacking the superiority pillar is two fold; build yourself up and knock us down and soon this pillar will come crashing down.

7.5 Toppling the Pillar of Lack of Accountability

If you are advancing your revenge campaign and have approached it by assaulting the pillars in the order detailed above, you are now at the halfway point and ready to look to topple the four remaining pillars. Our famed lack of accountability comes next. How do you attack this pillar?

You need to make us account for things that we have done which are wrong in environments where someone else will effect the need for us to be accountable. You cannot make us accountable even if your try to do so in an unemotional manner. You need to turn to third parties who are able to wield a greater degree of power than you. Now, ordinarily we would regard the involvement of the authorities and/or regulatory bodies and the like as a challenge. We would welcome the attention, we are content to wriggle, squirm, lie and endeavour to escape the attempt to pin accountability on us. Ordinarily people try to achieve this when we are riding high. We have our primary source of fuel supplying us, we have copious amounts of fuel from supplementary sources, we deal with criticisms effectively using our ignited fury and we are able to replenish the fuel used to power this ignited fury easily. In such a position the involvement of the authorities does not both us at all. We will charm them, deny wrongdoing and deflect.

During a properly executed revenge campaign the scenario is entirely different. Charm is in limited supply and is refusing to stretch. Fuel is diminishing and sources of supply are scarce. We are forced to shield ourselves as we try and repair the damage from the criticisms. Much like the way you are when you are in the middle of our maelstrom, we are now getting a dose of our medicine as we are caught up in the multiplicity of your attacks. In such a situation, when you utilise the assistance of third parties we find ourselves backed into a corner and ultimately we are forced to account for the things we have done or ought to have done or face further penalty.

Accordingly, in the way you did so when you attacked our status you should advise our workplace (where deemed appropriate), clubs, societies, regulatory bodies and so forth of any legitimate transgressions which we should account for. Once done and evidence provided, let them go to work.

Where we have committed criminal acts involve the police. Report us to the revenues for tax shortcomings, utilise the relevant enforcement body when child support has not been paid and any other appropriate body where we have acted incorrectly through commission or omission. Suitably weakened these further criticisms delivered by people in a non-fuel providing way will hurt us further. We cannot lash out and try and provoke you, as you are one step removed from the process.

Maintain the pressure by organising those of your supporters who are reliable to ask us in a neutral fashion to explain our actions with reference to our behaviour. Usually we would fight back and deny or use one of our other manipulative tactics to deal with this criticism and provoke a reaction but in this weakened condition as our various pillars are assailed we either cannot do so or our effectiveness is much reduced. We will still not explain ourselves (so if you think you will get some answer you will be disappointed) but these parties on your behalf will be landing even more blows as these questions are critical of our behaviour. We are slipping and sliding.

From your perspective you may wish to carry out similar actions face to face subject to how comfortable you are with doing so and whether you can deal with the Hoover (albeit most likely a weak one) that shall appear. If you decide against as face-to-face scenario you can still land blows using e-mails and social media. On social media you can make unemotional announcements such as

"He abused me for six years. He knows he has done wrong. Accountable."

"He treated me terribly. He knows what he did. Accountable."

Your supporters will rally behind these messages. We will see them or have them brought to our attention. These matter of fact statements, which contain no emotion, will wound us with the criticism contained therein. We may try and fight back by replying. If that happens ensure you and your supporters do not engage in any form of discussion, even if it lacks emotion. Instead just keep repeating the original message like a mantra. Each time you do you are driving a critical knife into us and we are unable to do anything. You can do similar by sending e-mails. As advised above you may like to create a specific account such as accountable@yahoo.com or heldtoaccount@gmail.com or such like. Using this platform, you can e-mail us and write

"You have done wrong. You will be held to account for your actions."

"You have committed many wrong acts. You are accountable."

Once again any engagement by us should be met by a repetition of this message. Resist the urge to gloat or crow as this will provide fuel and we very much need this.

When you have sent numerous e-mails along these lines you should change tack slightly and send messages stating

"You took money from me. Tell me about it."

"You broke my arm. Tell me about it."

"You spat in my face at dinner. Tell me about it."

"You stopped me seeing my friends. Tell me about it."

Do not write things such as you hurt me or you made my life hell, that is allowing emotion. Stick to factual statements and invite us to tell you about it. This is forcing us to confront what we have done. In the position that we are in we want to argue with you, point out how you are wrong, how it was your fault, how you made us do it, how we had a bad day at work. You have heard it all before. Now we will struggle to do so. We most likely will not reply but you will have landed a further criticism against us. If we do respond you may even start to get some form of diluted apology as a consequence of our weakened position. We are playing a pity card and looking to evoke sympathy as a last chance act. Do not reply to whatever we write. Instead you can secretly delight that you have thrust the critical knife deep into us and twisted it.

By doing these things the pillar of lack of accountability will be cracking and soon topple.

7.6 Toppling the Pillar of Projection

Toppling the pillar of projection or blame shifting is done in one way. This pillar rests on a foundation of it always being your fault. When we apply this manipulative technique you are caught in the crossfire of so much of our push and pull behaviour, you cannot make sense of what is going on and you are utterly confused and bewildered. You cannot understand why we keep saying that it is your fault when surely it is obvious that it is not. When we blame-shift you do not know what we are, you do not know what fuel is and you do not know that you are being manipulated. When you effect a revenge campaign not only do you know all of those things but also you are in a much stronger place. Your mind is clearer, your resolve is steeled, you are rested, supported and you have a clarity of purpose. The manipulations are now spotted as they happen. You have read my books on all the various subjects and therefore you know why I do as I do, what the intention is and how you can negate it. The fog of battle has cleared away and you stand before the pillar of projection, sledgehammer in hand.

The actual act of toppling this tower is not especially difficult. The difficulty lies in being able to crawl out of the chaos that obscured this target and then knowing where the target is. We purposefully unleashed so much trauma and chaos against you that you could not function and therefore even if you knew about this pillar you could not reach it, target it or muster enough strength to even dent it. That has all changed. With the clarity afforded by rest and understanding, with the will aided by support and help, you have cleared a way through the fog and you are ready to deal a critical blow to this pillar.

To do this you repeatedly assert that you are not to blame. You can do so in person, trumpet it through social media, and use third parties to do it, send it in letters and/or e-mails. The message as ever remains simple and without emotion.

"I am not to blame for what you did."

"I did nothing wrong."

"I never did anything wrong."

"I am blameless for your behaviour."

Straight to the point comments of this nature are all that are required. Do not engage in any response but merely restate the message. We know what we have done but we always got away with it because we made you think it was your fault. Now you know you did nothing wrong the obvious criticism that we are the guilty party slams hard against this pillar. You show us that you are realising the truth. We have become weakened and lack the means to try and convince you otherwise. Your direct and unemotional statement of fact tears into us and the pillar of projection comes crashing down as we realise we can longer manipulate you in this manner.

7.7 Toppling the Pillar of Lack of Empathy

Could it be that the key to toppling this pillar lies in getting us to feel empathy? The short answer to that question is no. We are not created to feel empathy and that is not going to change now as the pillars crash to the ground. By placing us in this weakened state, by criticising us and attacking our status, our entitlement, our omnipotence and so on, what is the one thing that we are crying out for? Yes, fuel of course but in what form do we want it to appear? Absolutely correct. We want to feel that empathy for which you are so well known. We are weakened, we are hurting, the situation is unfair and this harsh world is driving us towards the abyss. We need to be saved. We need the hurting to stop. Please make it stop. This is what you do isn't it? You fix, you heal but most of all you flow with empathy for someone else's situation, notably when they are hurt and in distress. We will play pity cards, lie through our teeth, twist and flail as we scream for you to give us empathy and thus fuel us so the damage of all this criticism can be repaired. We are so desperate for your empathic ways we will promise all sorts, we will seek treatment, we will change, we are sorry, we are so sorry for everything that we have done and everything we should have done. You have heard this all before. It formed a Power Play during the Grand Hoover and you fell for it. Back then you were weak. Back then you were uninformed. Back then you had not seized the power through reading my books. That has all changed. Back then you readily fell for our pretence as we limped and pretended to be contrite and injured so that we could drink deep from your empathic Hoover fuel. Not so any longer. Now you deal with our frenetic attempts to get you to show some empathy towards us in two ways: -

1.   You show empathy as usual to everyone else. In fact, you ensure that all your empathic acts are heralded to the world. Acts of kindness become plastered on facebook,

"Helped a homeless man today with his belongings and gave him a warm meal."

"Donated some unwanted belongings to the red cross" (Wonder what those items were?)

"Great day at the animal shelter. Rex is on the mend."

"Running in the London Marathon for Cancer UK and looking for sponsorship."

"Signed up to help youngster with learning difficulties by volunteering at a local school."

"Looked after my gran today as she was feeling unwell."

Show us what we are missing. Let the empathy flow over every one else. Treat us like a parched man who has crawled through the desert and you are holding a bottle of ice cold water in front of us and then pass it someone else. Your usual weaknesses that arise from being so empathic will not be as difficult to keep under control because you are: -

a.   No longer in the confusing maelstrom;

b.   Free of our influence;

c.   Stronger through recovery; and

d.   Of a harder heart owing to your resolve to seek revenge.

Thus let the empathy flow for everyone else.

2.   Do not give any empathy to us. As we beg and plead do not react. Do not mock or become upset but just look at us with an expressionless face. This will tear us apart as we recall how easily we use to get the empathic fuel from you and now you are denying it to us when our need is greatest. You must truly have no feelings for us. We will try and tell ourselves that you hate and despise us and although that may be true you are not showing it and therefore this last gasp attempt to garner some fuel will fail. The lack of emotion and the refusal to provide us with the empathy we need when we are hurting will bring this pillar crashing down.

7.8 Toppling the Pillar of Attention Seeking

The final pillar. As mentioned previously, you may not be tackling this last but in conjunction with your assaults on all the other pillars. That is something I certainly recommend in order to make your revenge campaign as effective as possible. In demolishing this pillar you need once again to adopt a two-pronged approach: -

1.   Draw attention to yourself;

2.   Give none to us and ensure others do not.

As I have explained above we want the spotlight on us at all times and if it should ever wander away onto you we will do something to wrench it back towards us. When we held you in our grip you were fearful of doing anything which contravened what we wanted. That fear has now gone. In order to topple this pillar focus on such acts as: -

- Organising dinner parties, drinks receptions, nights out and ensuring that they are broadcast to demonstrate your popularity and the existence of your support networks

- If we have a shared social life involve all those people who can be trusted. We will see them as disloyal to us by spending time with you and this criticism that they prefer to be with you than us will wound us

- Ensure you organise events or attend events which we would have gone to but now you have engineered so we are not invited or we are excluded

- Show how you have recovered, what you are achieving and how you are progressing but most of all show that you have an audience

- Where you are able, present evidence of what has happened to people and allow them to make a decision. Dealt with in this unemotional and factual fashion you are more likely to have people turn against us or at the very least not want to bother with us anymore. This will wound us.

- Never react to anything we do, ignore invitations, ask your support network to assist you in boycotting anything we might organise in order to gain attention

- Ignore drama that we create no matter how severe it may sound. Remind yourself of the relevant Power Plays from No Contact and be aware of them so you do not respond to these attempts to gain attention

- If it is something you enjoy, engage in performances with amateur dramatics and be involved with performances. Look to arrange coverage of the performance.

- Again if it something you enjoy become involved in competitive activities, either individual or team based and ensure that victories and achievements are broadcast

- Recognise that your other actions against other pillars will have a knock on effect in terms of diminishing the attention we command. Our weakened state means we will lack the critical faculties to gather attention as we once did and thus we enter a downward spiral.

Keep ensuring we know how popular and well liked you are, and whilst doing this look to keep the spotlight away from us for you own part and others who are supportive of the action you are taking. Doing this will bring this pillar down also.

8 Prohibited Revenge Conduct

Before I explain to you what is left as the dust settles following the collapse of the relevant number of narcissistic pillars, it is worth a brief mention of things you should not do when effecting your revenge campaign.

- Do not break the law. This will derail your campaign and we will seize this own goal with great gladness in order to stop what you are doing against us. It may be tempting to smash the windows on our car or daub hateful graffiti on the side of our house but you must not take such steps. You will only create trouble for yourself and a golden opportunity for us to derail your campaign, recover from the damage you have inflicted and allow us to avoid your revenge because we will know what you were doing.

- Do not expose yourself to defamation claims by posting, circulating, saying or stating untruths. Again this is an own goal and one we will jump on, as we will take action against you as this provides us with an escape route from your revenge campaign. We will take legal action against you, which will derail your campaign and could prove costly for you.

- Never expose yourself to the risk of physical danger. You know the nature of the narcissist you are dealing with. Much of the steps I have advanced are ones, which are done through third parties or indirectly from a distance. There are instances where face-to face contact can bring results but this should only be done when there is no risk to you.

- Similarly, do not commence the revenge campaign if you have not sufficiently recovered and you do not feel strong enough. You may harm yourself, make yourself susceptible to a successful Hoover and you campaign fails.

- Do not commence a revenge campaign without support. You need it for all the reasons detailed above.

- Do not try to convince us of our wrongdoing. No matter how successful your campaign may be progressing this will not work.

- Do not try to fix us. It cannot be done.

- Do not place emotive advertisements, placards, billboards etc attacking us. It is fuel, you will look stupid and you will lose valuable support.

- Do not interfere in contractual relations, e.g. changing bookings on our behalf, ordering things in our name and such like. This will provide us with grounds to complain about you and potentially provide an actionable basis to take legal action against you. This will be an own goal.

- Do not lose sight of the targets. Do not be distracted by what we might do to try and deflect you, convince you to stop or otherwise dissuade you.

- Do not show emotion.

9 So What is Next?

By removing our means of obtaining fuel from you because you have conducted your campaign in accordance with the Core Principle you will have weakened us and also prevented a means by which we might gain some strength as you attack us. You may have pulled off the coup of removing the new primary source of fuel, which will be a devastating blow against. Your actions will also no doubt have diminished our supplementary sources. If you had just affected our fuel supply, we would retreat and replenish by finding new sources and the strike back at you.

You however have not stopped there. With the fuel supplies seriously damaged, you have then rained down blow after blow against us through the application of repeated critical acts. Criticism, as you know, wounds us deeply. This has ignited our fury but the damage to our fuel supplies means we cannot use fury as a weapon against you. The sustained nature of your campaign means we cannot retreat and seek to recover. Instead we have no choice but to use this ignited fury to repair the holes you have smashed in the construct. Ordinarily this would allow us to recover and then we would turn to sources of fuel in order to replenish that which has been used up to power the shield. That opportunity has been taken away from us. The removal of fuel and also the holes you have punched in our construct means that those shards and segments, which we use to attract, seduce and ensnare, are being lost. Our capability to attract new fuel is being lost. You are not providing us with fuel, we cannot get it elsewhere (or at least not in sufficient quantities) and you are damaging our ability to attract new sources. You continue to land criticisms against us, as we are too weak to fight back. We cannot use our various manipulations like we once did to try and deflect you or ensnare you.

The blows are causing the pillars to come crashing down. The very central characteristics that define what we are are being torn down, smashed down and obliterated. All of the things that we believe we are, all of the artifice that we have created to show the world beyond is being destroyed. The pillars that supported our magnificent palace tumble and the glorious structure crashes to the ground. The construct, with so many holes smashed into it by your criticisms collapses as these pillars collapse. Our identity has been lost. You have destroyed what we believed ourselves to be. You have annihilated that which we showed the world and it cannot be recovered. All that you have left behind, now freed from its bondage behind the construct and the pillars is the wretched creature. Our true self.

How will you recognise what this is? It is simple enough. It is what is left behind after all the traits afforded by the pillars and the stolen shards and segments have been removed. Gone is the confidence. Gone is the boasting. Gone is the charm. All those traits that are allowed by the existence of the pillars have been taken away and you will be left with whom we really are, a weak and fragile creature that will slink away from you. He cannot remain in the world any longer and must depart the kingdom he once rules and be sent into self-imposed exile away from his destroyer, away from his minions and his lieutenants, away from his other victims. When you succeed in toppling the pillars you will know when success has been achieved by the very thing that stands before you. Something, which you have never seen before yet someone you had known for so long.

Who or what is this creature? That forms the basis of a different publication but you have succeeded. The narcissist has been destroyed and you have achieved the ultimate aim. You have secured your revenge.

10 Conclusion

A successful revenge campaign is not easy. You must make suitable preparation and follow what has been detailed in this book in order to secure your revenge. You must understand what revenge is and what it looks like. You must know the foe you are dealing with. You must always abide by the Core Principle otherwise your actions will be ineffective and then we are likely to counter-attack and derail your campaign. You must understand the pillars and what they represent so you know where to aim and you must know how to topple those pillars. You must act in a sustained fashion, maintaining the campaign otherwise it will not work. Through this you will destroy the narcissist and leave only the wretched creature behind. What of me? All this talk of revenge has reminded me I must go and check that all my pillars are strong and intact, so you must excuse me. Farewell.

Evil

Narcissist: Seduction

Narcissist: Ensnared

Manipulated

Confessions of a Narcissist

More Confessions of a Narcissist

Further Confessions of a Narcissist

From the Mouth of a Narcissist

Escape: How to Beat the Narcissist

Danger: 50 Things You Should Not Do With a
Narcissist

Departure Imminent: Preparing for No Contact to beat
the Narcissist

Fuel

Chained: The Narcissist's Co-Dependent

A Delinquent Mind

Fury

Beautiful and Barbaric

The Devil's Toolkit

Sex and the Narcissist

Treasured and Tormented

No Contact: How to Beat the Narcissist

All available on Amazon

Further interaction with H G Tudor

Knowing the Narcissist

@narcissist_me

Facebook

Narcsite.wordpress.com

Made in United States
North Haven, CT
12 March 2024

49900679R00085